BANGKOK
73

The tone and character of Uppsala showed that we are in a new age. The "wind of change" has become a hurricane.

Reports from Uppsala 1968, p. xx

We are at the end of a missionary era and at the very beginning of the world mission.

Emilio Castro, Bangkok 1973

And this gospel of the kingdom shall be preached in all the world for a witness unto all nations; and then shall the end come.

Matthew 24:14

BANGKOK 73

The beginning or end of world mission?

Peter Beyerhaus

ZONDERVAN
PUBLISHING HOUSE
OF THE ZONDERVAN CORPORATION
GRAND RAPIDS, MICHIGAN 49506

BANGKOK '73
by Peter Beyerhaus

Copyright © 1973 by the publishing house of the Liebenzell Mission,
Bad Liebenzell

English Edition copyright © 1974 by The Zondervan Corporation

Library of Congress Catalog Card Number 74-4949

Printed in the United States of America

To

Rudolph Baumer and Paul Deitenbeck
at the completion of 60 years
in brotherly fellowship!

CONTENTS

FOREWORD

Ours is an age of conferences and consultations. Because of the recent technological revolution, the historic barriers of space and language are no longer as formidable as they once were. At the same time the improved means of interchange have focused attention both on the issues that divide mankind and on the compelling necessity to do something about these problems in light of the growing interdependence of the world. In our century it has been assumed that one effective way to deal with this situation is to call a conference. The hope is that discussion by those primarily concerned will provide opportunity for a more precise definition of subject matter and an improved understanding that will in turn lead to agreement on a program of action.

While there has been some success in the use of this procedure, there have also been spectacular failures. In either case the determining factor seems to be the degree to which the participants are able to concur in what the issues are and, more importantly, what the principles are which govern the development of appropriate solutions. Despite improved means of communication the barriers to effective interchange through conferences, particularly those involving world-wide participation, are still much in evidence. Cultural and national loyalties are extraordinarily robust and are not easily set aside in favor of less provincial considerations. Only when a gathering can be summoned to a common denominator of purpose is there any hope of significant achievement.

The Bangkok Conference addressed itself to a manifest need: salvation today. There has scarcely been a time in the world's history when deliverance is more desired than at present. Yet in retrospect it has become evident that Bangkok '73 lacked the ingredient essential to meaningful action.

As a participant Professor Beyerhaus had the advantage of firsthand observation. The time since the conference has also furnished him with the interval necessary to develop an appropriate perspective. What he has written identifies the reason why Bangkok could not measure up to the hopes and expectations generated by its theme. There was a basic difference of opinion about the nature of salvation. Both the planning and the procedures were oriented primarily toward temporal concerns. Indeed, for all practical purposes the immediate needs of men, admittedly important became transcendant and eclipsed those related to eternal destiny.

This was no accident. On the contrary, it was the necessary product of the view of truth held by those who convened the conference. Rather than the Holy Scriptures being of timeless significance and normative in their statements about God, man, sin and redemption, they were perceived as descriptive of but one set of historic events and convictions not necessarily pertinent for today. Hence, a reformulation of salvation that inverted the Biblical priorities was considered not only possible but also necessary in light of alleged changing circumstances in our time. Yet it was also recognized that a gathering that was pluralistic in its views could easily become polarized without some reference point. Hence, Bible studies were scheduled.

Professor Beyerhaus has called attention to the fact, however, that whether by open disavowal or by a clever hermeneutic the Bible was not in fact the basis on which conclusions were reached at Bangkok. Instead, there was the employment of techniques that elevated shared experiences to the place of preeminence in the achievement of consensus.

This discloses a basic problem in the ecclesiastical world today. Part of the attraction of those forms of religious expression that stress experience is that it gives priority to the emotional over the rational and seems to eliminate disagreements over doctrine that have divided believers. Unfortunately, such a stress on experience at the expense of Biblical truth sacrifices objectivity and stability and removes any effective criterion of reality. It thus opens the way for manipulation and condemns man to an unending quest for assurance and hope that can never be realized in this manner.

We are indebted to Professor Beyerhaus for his delineation of the real issue at Bangkok, for it reflects the current dilemma of the professing community. Evangelicals need to recognize that unity at the expense of truth is not only futile but also impossible. At the same time, they now have both the opportunity and the responsibility to declare that there is indeed Salvation Today as defined by the Scriptures and as centered in the redeeming work of Christ upon the cross. Such a declaration necessarily locates its authority in Biblical revelation rather than experience, however meaningful. Unless the word is from God its authenticity is subject to challenge and contradiction.

This book, then, is more than a chronicle or a critique. It is a call to the evangelical community to affirmation and action. It should be heeded since it recalls us all to the only true basis for salvation today: the Word of God.

Hudson T. Armerding
President, Wheaton College

PREFACE

IT IS NOT MY intention in this book to add yet another report to the many dealing with the conference on "Salvation Today." Nor is it my concern as one of the 326 participants there to give a complete picture of my experiences and encounters in Bangkok. Neither do I intend to provide an overview of the many opinions on the conference, shared or personal, which were heard and observed there and which will certainly be of deep concern to us for a long time. The composition of the conference and the range of official and unofficial records were too diverse to enable me to do all these things.

I would also like to admit freely that I am not in a position to reduce all that was said in Bangkok to one common theological denominator; that strikes me as impossible. Again, I would like to make it clear at the outset that I am thankful for the many good things that went on at Bangkok in worship services, Bible studies, and section meetings and which were partially reflected in the official report. I grew closer to many people through personal fellowship in those days and I am particularly happy about that.

But these things are not the occasion for this work. It is rather my concern to share with the reader a profound uneasiness about certain pervasive signs in this ecumenical event which could be of disastrous consequence for the future of missions, for Christianity, and probably even for all mankind. I therefore feel constrained to address myself in this work to all Christians who are responsibly thinking and praying about missions.

Beneath my uneasiness lies a fully positive desire: I want to give readers information and a theological interpretation about the World Conference in Bangkok that can equip them — precisely here in the face of the error and deceiving force of this conference — to see more clearly than ever before their own biblically grounded responsibility for the spread of the Gospel in all the world. It can also help them make the critical judgments that are going to be necessary if this is to be done.

For the failure of Bangkok, which in its essentials this volume will describe, is in no sense the failure of the world mission of Jesus Christ. And agreement by many mission leaders on a novel program of missions that is no longer worthy of the name can hardly prevent Christ from calling and equipping other witnesses through whom He will bring His missionary task to completion. For in the sense of Matthew 24:14, chosen as an epigraph of this book, we may be fully confident of these things: that the salvation of a world lost in the guilt of its sins (a salvation won in Jesus' passion on the cross) and Jesus' victory over the powers of death and the devil (won on Easter morning) will be proclaimed farther over the whole earth until all people have heard the Gospel, and that He Himself will return to display His triumph even to those who would not believe. Then every knee will bow and every tongue will confess that Jesus is Lord for the glory of God the Father (Phil. 2:11).

This book is made up of two major parts. The first part offers a comprehensive and reflective description of my impressions of the World Conference. For this book I have taken pains to study thoroughly the literature on Bangkok that has subsequently come to my attention. At the same time, it is on the basis of a thorough study of the practice of *Sensitivity Training* that I wish to establish my main thesis: the most important thing to grasp concerning the troubling events at Samut Prakan (the conference center in Bangkok) is that the organizers were conducting an experiment in group dynamics. In my opinion this is the most important discovery I made during the conference. For that reason the longest chapter is devoted to it.

The second part of the book provides detailed documentation for my *second thesis*: Bangkok's understanding of salvation and missions was not the biblical one but rather a syncretistic and social-political one; and further, where the Bible was apparently used, Christian assertions were ideologically undermined.

It could be contended that, given the point of view taken in the first part of the book, the documents, as presented, may seem one-sided and torn from their contexts. It is, of course, the essence of quotation to take something out of its context. Yet I have taken pains to present citations as comprehensively as possible. To the charge of one-sidedness I respond that I am consciously placing those comments about the conference stemming from evangelicals next to the most radical witnesses of the ecumenical theology believing that these latter are truly representative of Bangkok and are those that point the way for the future course of the ecumenical Commission for World Mission and Evangelism. The evangelical testimonies include, for example, the "Affirmation on Salvation Today" which came from Bible Study Group 3 and the report of Subsection II B, "Growing Churches and Renewal," the most evangelical of all the subsections. I myself was a member of this subsection and contributed a short report to it. My contribution appears in the Bangkok Report as a supplement acknowledged by the section but for which they assumed no responsibility.

I am indeed convinced that these conservative-evangelical notes in the Bangkok concert do not alter the nature of this ecumenical composition, but can at the most give it an apparent respectability before an evangelical public. And for that reason the whole matter is even more dangerous. I would not, in view of this danger, take part in such an undertaking again. For in a situation like this the Church of Christ takes on a pluralistic aspect: theological heresies and non-Christian ideologies are granted equal right to stand beside biblical truth, or sometimes everything is jumbled together into an ecumenical tossed salad. And that is much worse than a massive attack by an opponent openly combatting biblical truth. If there is one rotten egg, the whole cake will be inedible, even if the other nine eggs are fresh.

The mission of Jesus Christ is not served today by a passionate will-to-action that despises clear differences in doctrine or by an experience of group dynamics sentimentally glossing over the contemporary crisis in theological foundations. But these attitudes have been elevated to dogma under the current Geneva administration of the World Council of Churches. Christ's mission requires much more than this — first and foremost, a passionate wrestling for biblical truth. For this truth alone will make us and those who hear our missionary message — free.

BANGKOK
73

THE REPORT

1

WHAT IS MEANT BY "SALVATION" IN THE BANGKOK MOTTO "SALVATION TODAY"?

THE THEME FOR THE Eighth Conference on World Mission, "Salvation Today," was announced shortly after the General Assembly of the World Council of Churches (WCC) held at Uppsala, Sweden, in 1968. How was the slogan chosen? The constitution of the Commission for World Mission and Evangelism of the WCC, established in New Delhi in 1961 and with which almost all national mission councils of the world are affiliated, states that its mandate is to work "to further the proclamation to the whole world of the Gospel of Jesus Christ to the end that all men may believe in him and be saved." Here, as in the tradition of the international missions movement arising from the great revivals of the 18th and 19th centuries, "salvation," bestowed on those who believe in the message of salvation proclaimed in Jesus Christ, was the goal. Our predecessors' understanding of this salvation, that is, "redemption" or "deliverance," was always unequivocal because of their firm commitment to Holy Scripture. It was the deliverance of sinners from the wrath of God, including both present reconstitution of fellowship with Him through the forgiveness of human guilt and also acquittal at the Judgment Day:

> Your passion saved the world; by strife beset
> yet innocent, you payed our debt.
> Our champion, our sure guide to heaven — we raise
> to you a joyful hymn of praise.
>
> CHRISTOPH G. BARTH
> German Protestant Hymnbook, #222

But just two years after accepting such a gratifyingly biblical statement of purpose, it became apparent that this very understanding of salvation was being called into question by the now ecumenically aligned mission agencies. At least this was true of spokesmen for this group. In the report of the Seventh World Missionary Conference in Mexico City we read, for example, the perplexing question "What is the form and content of the salvation which Christ offers men in the secular world?"[1] To the extent that the impetus for thinking about missions was no longer taken from biblical principles but from the thought of contemporary men in a changed world, there was a corresponding questioning by these ecumenical mission leaders not only of the form but also of the content of the salvation given to us in Christ. In that same year, 1963, a defender of the Confessing Church in Germany could even declare that the question posed by contemporary man is no longer the question asked by Martin Luther — "How can I get right with God?" The question now is rather "How can I get right with my fellowman?" This certainly reveals a reversal in the crucial dimension in which salvation is understood. The concept has changed from the vertical to the horizontal, that is, from the basic relationship between God and man to the social connections of humanity.

The thinking which was expressed only suggestively as a question in Mexico in 1963 broke out into open conflict five years later at Uppsala. In Uppsala, in the second section, whose assignment was to treat the subject "Renewal in Mission," so-called horizontalists and verticalists, otherwise designated as ecumenicals and evangelicals, suddenly emerged in an open dispute as passionate as it was lacking in mutual comprehension of the issues. Evangelicals sought to hold fast to the priority of preaching, repentance, rebirth, and the establishment of churches as the content and goal of missions for the future. Ecumenicals, by contrast, proclaimed "humanization," so-called, as the only sensible goal of missions today. By this they meant the humanization of social and political relationships in the strife-torn areas of society. Dialogue and also, in certain circumstances, participation in the revolutionary movements of our time were said to mark the path to this goal. All these, it was stated, are likewise part of that *Missio Dei* which goes far beyond the church's traditional forms of outreach, that Mission of God which is being worked out in world history. God can go beyond the church to get His business done by using Marxists, humanists, and members of other religions.[2]

The conflict at Uppsala led missions-minded believers to sound a worldwide alarm. World missions was being polarized ever more thor-

---

[1] Theodor Müller-Krüger, ed., *In sechs Kontinenten* [*In Six Continents*] (Stuttgart, 1964), p. 161.
[2] Cf. my booklet, "Humanisierung — einzige Hoffnung der Welt?" ["Humanization — the only hope of the world?"] (Bad Salzuflen, 2nd edition, 1970).

oughly into two opposing camps. When all was said and done, the issue dividing them was their fundamentally conflicting views on the nature of salvation. It became progressively clearer that ecumenically organized missions were in the throes of a deep and fundamental theological crisis. This crisis arose, first, because confidence in the validity of Holy Scripture as the sole guide of Christian missions was shaken, and, second, because concepts of salvation that are contrary to the Gospel and owe their existence to the ideologies and religions of our own time had infiltrated the movement.

The most deceptive aspect of this crisis was, without doubt, that although these novel ideas were expressed in frankly ideological terms such as "humanization, identity, dialogue, revolution," etc., they also and much more importantly were expressed in a biblical phraseology which, however, had been secretly given a totally altered meaning. It was for this reason that many ordinary Christians, although feeling a growing uneasiness about these movements, did not fully realize that a great change was taking place in the missions enterprises which they were still being urged to support. The nature of this change first became clear when the WCC instituted its antiracism program in September, 1970; in the following two years posters for the "Information Campaign for World Missions" in Germany openly solicited support for a totally altered set of mission goals.

Earlier, however, theologians and missionary leaders loyal to Scripture had sounded the alarm with the "Frankfurt Declaration on the Fundamental Crisis in Christian Missions."[3] Within a few short months this document found a remarkable response on all six continents; it opened the eyes of many church leaders, missionaries, church officials, and church members to the earthquake that had begun to shake the foundations, the content, and the aims of missions. All these people — whether Germans, Norwegians, Americans, Indians, Indonesians, or Japanese — quickly perceived that the description of the indispensable but threatened foundations of missions in the seven theses and condemnations of the Frankfurt Declaration was also a strikingly accurate description of the events taking place in their own churches and mission agencies as a result of the influence of the ecumenical movement. The Frankfurt Declaration was, as a consequence, translated immediately into the most important European and Asian languages; it was discussed by church and mission leaders and at centers of theological education.

I would like to make it altogether clear at this point that the Frank-

---

[3] Cf. my booklet, "Die Grundlagenkrise der Mission" ["The Fundamental Crisis of Missions"] (Rolf Brockhaus Verlag, 1970).

furt Declaration was not in any way intended originally as an appeal for separation from the Geneva Commission on World Mission or from the mission councils and societies associated with it. To the contrary, the Declaration expressed a constructive desire for a biblical and theological clarification of the course pursued by these missions; it sought to recall Christian world missions to a proper emphasis on salvation history.

In light of this concern the selection of the theme for Bangkok was at first hailed even by those missionary agencies all over the world that are loyal to Scripture. It was hoped that joint labor on the main theme, "Salvation Today," would perforce provide an opportunity to recover from the shock of Uppsala. If such a conference could make biblically responsible pronouncements on the essence of missions, a way could be opened out of the crisis in principles and public confidence and into a new cooperative drive in the world missionary movement. And so people everywhere got right to work. Study groups were formed all over the world and training institutes were set up to prepare people thoroughly for the anticipated missionary conference. In fact, the flood of materials pouring into Geneva was so voluminous and the attendant difficulties in sorting through them were so great that the conference had to be postponed repeatedly from its originally scheduled opening in December, 1969, to its final date in late 1972 and early 1973.

Although the exchange of information among the various groups was regrettably slight, there was sufficient evidence to indicate that among the reports contributed were several very good works, and this in spite of an unbelievable contrast in theological seriousness and Christian integrity evident in the range of the reports. For example, I received the report of the Norwegian study group from Oslo, a report based on masterful biblical and theological labor by the Swedish New Testament scholar, Edvin Larsson. It was highly regrettable that the exegetical conclusions of this publication were not promptly distributed. In addition, no summary of the areas of agreement and disagreement was provided; this could have stimulated concentrated study.

It was clear already from these preliminary works that the participants had completely different interpretations of the theme. Encounter between representatives of the two views — namely, proponents of the biblical testimony on salvation and those who focused on the concrete situations of the recipients of the message — was used as a method of preparation and also as the method for organizing the conference. In this, however, we actually began to see a division into three groups. The first group took its point of departure essentially from the statements of Holy Scripture which it saw as the directing and normative authority also for the attainment of salvation today. The second group was already so deeply engaged in political and social efforts to change modern society that it was hardly able to muster time or interest for the study of Scripture. This group even called into question the place of personal faith in Jesus Christ as an indispensable prerequisite for salvation. Finally, a *third* group was made up of the practitioners of modern biblical scholarship and in particular those who stressed a historical-critical methodology. To be sure, they were like the first group in taking their point of departure from study of the Old and New Testaments. But in so doing they promulgated such contradictory interpretations of the texts under discussion that they only added to the general ecumenical confusion.

In this confusion we certainly see the profoundest source of the tragedy at Bangkok, and indeed in the ecumenical movement altogether. And the spiritual error and confusion of the ecumenical movement arose in turn from the fundamental crisis in the view of Scripture found in the theology of its member churches.

The preliminary investigation of the theme "Salvation Today" was to have constructed a bridge on the twin piles of Scripture and the contemporary situation (that is, experience). Needless to say, difficulties which had not been anticipated quickly appeared to hamper the project. The two sides of the equation proposed in the formula "Scripture and Experience" refused to admit equality. In an interim report distributed in July, 1971, Thomas Wieser, the Geneva official in charge of the study project "Salvation Today," complained about "a growing difference of meaning in the concepts used to understand salvation as the content and goal of missions. At the same time," he said, "it now seems less and less probable that we will succeed in reaching an ecumenical concensus by the help of this study."[4] Ecumenical pluralism, revealed here as a crippling influence on theology, affected first the exegetical studies of the biblical concept of salvation. These studies showed, it was said, that there is simply no one central understanding of salvation in the Old and New Testaments from which all practical descriptions of salvation could be consistently derived. Rather, there were any number of different concepts of salvation in the individual biblical writings — personal and community salvation, corporeal and spiritual, this-wordly and other-worldly. It was further claimed that these are distinct from each other; some are in harmony with the others, some are not. The Geneva headquarters apparently did not realize that, where this issue was concerned, it had not so much run

---

[4] *Das Wort in der Welt [The Word in the World]*, no. 4 (1971), p. 114.

into a difficulty in the matter under consideration, but that it had instead blundered into the undertow of the fundamental hermeneutical crisis in modern exegesis. The principles of Scripture interpretation, that is, hermeneutics, have for some time suffered from the effects of the rationalistic Enlightenment.[5]

The Ecumenical Institute in Tübingen had participated in this study, as it had previously in preparation for Uppsala. It sent its own presentation to Geneva. This study contained five hermeneutical observations on the material that had already been produced. These observations are important as manifestations of the contemporary attitude to the Bible held by ecumenical theology:

(1) The Bible is only human testimony to the revelation of God, but not the binding thrust of that revelation itself.

(2) The great variety of biblical writings, sources, and editorial levels allows these human testimonies concerning God's revelation to appear contradictory to each other.

(3) Among the testimonies to salvation experiences the declarations of the Old Testament and New Testament are on the same plane and largely unrelated to each other. A contemporary salvation experience, or an expectation of salvation, can therefore be regarded as biblically based, if it conforms to any historical experiences of the old covenant people, Israel — for example, the political Exodus-motif (the passage of Israel from Egypt) — even if such a political event cannot be established as a Christian experience of salvation from the standpoint of the New Testament. (This line of thinking was prominent in the use of the Bible at Bangkok.) The ecumenical understanding of Scripture traces God's revelation and the history of His salvation action backwards: from the New Testament to the Old, from Christ to Moses.

(4) The Bible does not provide us with an eternally valid picture of the salvation message but only with a series of translations which have been adjusted to the time-bound notions and variable circumstances of the people who heard and read the message. Biblical passages, therefore can be made meaningful only if they are translated anew in light of our modern conditions; these translations transform not only the form of the language but even the content itself so that it too can be experienced as salvational.

(5) The Bible's testimony to revelation is not on an essentially different level than testimonies to the saving work of the same God outside the biblical history of election and in Christian history after the biblical era.

[5] Cf. P. Beyerhaus, *Bibel ohne Heiligen Geist?* [*Bible Without the Holy Spirit?*] (Bad Liebenzell, 3rd edition, 1970).

The capacity of the proposed exegetical piling of the Bangkok bridge to bear its own weight was thus seriously jeopardized by dividing revelation and Scripture, a division arising from dialectical theology. It was further jeopardized by the failure to grasp the organic relationship among the biblical writings themselves in their portrayal of salvation history, as well as by the abandonment of the finality of biblical and historical revelation in favor of situational and syncretistic commitments. ("Syncretism" means the mingling of religious bits and pieces from many sources.)

In order not to leave the exegetical part of the joint study in the lurch, a principle had to be found which could unite all these apparently disharmonious statements. Wieser finally discovered this principle in the pietistic concept of the "witness." A witness is not expected to reflect dogmatic clarity but only the genuineness of his own actual experience of salvation, an experience which in some way or other is also communicable and meaningful for people in situations of need that from time to time resemble his own. To be sure, the question whether this experience is credible as a biblically Christian experience of salvation had to be asked, but the answer was left up in the air. It was simply suggested that the experience of salvation should appeal to Jesus as its source.

If it is now asked where the interests of the majority of the Geneva staff directly responsible for conference planning lay and what position its ecumenical confidants all over the world maintained, it must be answered that they have to be classed in essentials with the second group named above, the group caring so much about the longing-for secular salvation in our day. Two observations made this evident to me.

The first came from listening to a tape from Geneva containing a discussion on "Salvation Today" by chief representatives of the ecumenical Commission on World Mission and Evangelism (CWME).[6] In this discussion the concept of salvation was discussed in its linguistic, political, and social aspects as well as in terms of the history of religions. None of the participants in the discussion by even a single word expressed awareness of the fact that in the biblical sense, salvation is first of all the reconciliation of the sinner with God on the basis of the sin-offering of Jesus Christ. Instead, such revealing comments as the following were spoken: "In Latin America . . . young people begin to see Che Guevara and Jesus Christ as belonging to the same tradition." Or again:

Through this kind of self-giving [as was practiced in Mao Tse-Tung's

6 See the documentary section: 1, C.

Cultural Revolution] the total historical progress will be moved onto
a new level of liberation and abundance for everybody entirely beyond
the bounds of formal Christianity but . . . reflecting profoundly the
operation of this spirit in history.

A book that appeared in February, 1972, under the title *Salvation
Today and Contemporary Experience* gave me another opportunity to
discover the peculiarly Genevan understanding of salvation. This book
is a collection of excerpts from contemporary works in the fields of
politics, pop music, modern literature, Marxist philosophy, and even
radical theology. These were said to articulate modern man's concern
for salvation. One of these testimonies is the report of a Red Chinese
under the title "Saved by Mao." Even more shocking is the concluding
piece, "The Priest and the Apostate," taken from a contemporary Japanese novel by Shusako Endo, *Silence*.[7] This contribution contends that
denial of belief in Christ for the sake of fellow prisoners during a time
of persecution is a realization of "Salvation Today"! The last sentence
in this anthology reads, significantly: "And far in the distance the cock
crew." This volume was the major preparatory document for Bangkok
and was especially recommended as such by the officials of the Department for World Mission and Evangelism (DWME).[8]

The book was sent to the Bangkok delegates and to the study groups
participating in the preparations with the request that they express
their opinion on it. Excerpts from these answers were then put into
the preparatory material for Bangkok and once again distributed. Besides much agreement, there was already at this stage serious criticism
from a few parties. The critics said that even if it is true that Christian
preaching and service must not be divorced from the needs and hopes
described in the anthology, that in no sense means that participation
in these areas of human life or even satisfying these kinds of demands
are the most pressing tasks of Christian missions. Rather, the criticism
went on, is it not true that this approach creates a specific danger —
that missions will simply be supplanted by the different problems of
modern contemporary society and the creation of party groupings to
confront these problems? Such indeed has already occurred, as the
slogan coined by Werner Simpfendorfer indicates: "The world deter-
mines the church's agenda." If the church lets this happen, will it not
lose sight of its commission and even the One who commissions, the

---

[7] Shusako Endo, *Silence* (Tokyo, 3rd edition, 1970); see the documentary
section: 1, B.

[8] *From Mexico City to Bangkok, Report of the Commission for World Mission
and Evangelism 1963-1972* (Geneva, 1972), p. 43.

One who sends out His Church on His mission? Can the desire for salvation as perceived by men really constitute a superior vantage point for the Christian message? On the contrary, does not the central message of judgment and grace in the cross involve first and foremost a serious question put by God to man rather than by man to God?

It is in this sense that the director of the Foreign Board of the Church of Norway, Gunnar Stalsett, argues concerning the preparatory volume:

> Salvation then is the answer to man's longing for welfare, peace, liberty, and happiness. Salvation is then more accurately to be expressed as "solution." But no one can today offer an instant solution to anyone with the deep problems indicated in our texts. . . . As compared with the biblical message of salvation, the term here loses its historic and ecumenical meaning, and salvation becomes exclusively situational. It becomes rather a quest for the solution of tomorrow than an offer of salvation today. Because the human cry is more or less uncritically accepted at face value, as a cry for salvation, salvation in Christ may be inferred to be that which answers the questions raised, whatever these questions deal with. This also may imply, or lead to the notion that universal history as such is salvation history. . . . If the questions as they are articulated in these texts are taken without further discussion as a cry for salvation, then every "trouble shooter" is a Savior. The task of the church in relation to the world in terms of salvation then becomes to register the needs and to satisfy them. And the answer to the needs may in each case be termed "gospel." Is not the whole central message of salvation in the Christian church in danger of being made void of its biblical and historic contents?[9]

These deeply penetrating objections from Norway are echoed by the criticism of our Tübingen Seminar. With such thoughts in mind I concluded my preview of Bangkok with questions that Hollenweger would later address in the first issue of the Bangkok conference newspaper, *Salvation Today*:

> The international missions movement stands again at the crossroads. Will the World Council's view of mission in the future really be based on the sort of pan-religious and humanistic-ideological understanding of salvation suggested by the preparatory documents? Or will it succeed in restoring the biblical and reformational emphasis which characterized the conferences at Madras (1938), Whitby (1947), and Willingen (1952) as well as the efforts of the leading missionary thinkers of those days such as Karl Hartenstein and Walter Freytag?[10]

[9] Mimeographed memorandum, "Solution Tomorrow or Salvation Today?"
[10] "Die Geister scheiden sich" ["The Spirits are Dividing"], *Evangelische Kommentare [Protestant Commentary]*, no. 12 (1973), p. 744.

In these questions I intentionally alluded to the constructive and critical role which, owing to their reformational appreciation of Scripture, the German delegations had exercised on many of the reports issued by the earlier World Mission Conferences. Of special note among these is the "German Declaration to the World Mission Conference in Tambaram" (Madras, 1938). Much in this declaration could be applied word for word as a criticism of the World Mission Conference in Bangkok, 1972/73. For that reason it is here quoted at length:

> But we are bound by conscience to point to some vital principles of the Gospel, which must be emphasized in contrast with certain passages in the reports of some sections.
>
> In the Apostles' Creed, we all confess together that Christ will come again to judge the living and the dead. In spite of the changes which have taken place in the aspect of the world and history since the days of the Apostles, we believe according to the scriptures that through a creative act of God His Kingdom will be consummated in the final establishment of a New Heaven and a New Earth. Christ has conquered for us sin and death and overcome the world, so that we share with Him His Eternal Life. But at the same time this our new life is hid with Christ in God. Sin, death, and Satan are still powers of reality in our world, and we live as citizens of two different orders, until Christ Himself will appear in power and glory to transform the whole structure of this world into His Kingdom of Righteousness and Victory.
>
> We are convinced that only this eschatological attitude can prevent the Church from becoming secularized. . . .
>
> The Church of Christ, being an interim-body between the times of God who has sent the Savior and will send Him again, is moving forward into this world to proclaim the redeeming message, that our sins are forgiven in Christ and we are saved by faith in hope. The Holy Spirit creates in this body the love of Christ, so that it is witnessing by word and deed in real brotherhood and sacrificial service for the sake of mankind. It cannot pass by the sufferings of the world, it is bound to comfort and heal the sick and downtrodden, to help and strengthen the poor and heavy-laden, to fight against injustice and social evils, to awaken the consciences of nations and mankind and so to be the light and the salt of the world. But being between the times the Church has not to bring into force a social program for a renewed world order, or even a Christian state. It cannot redeem the world from all inherent evils, but it serves and spends itself in promoting all good works in obedience to its God-given call. Expectation of the coming Lord and His Judgment means that the Church is always at work,

responsive to the tasks God offers daily, highly active in witnessing by word and deed, and so proclaiming the Lord's death till He comes.[11]

The German Protestant mission agencies certainly had the opportunity to raise their voices at Bangkok as Hartenstein, Freytag, Schlunk, and others had done at Tambaram. The German Protestant Missionary Council (Der Deutsche Evangelische Missionsrat) was represented by an official delegation of four leading missionary spokesmen, assisted and advised by six other German theologians as well as a group of seven journalists. The German Protestant Missionary Conference (Der Deutsche Evangelische Missionstag) was in fact intensively involved in preparations for the Bangkok conference at its Königsfeld mission week in October, 1972, as indicated by the conference theme "Salvation Today." The preparatory volume already discus̶ed, *Salvation Today and Contemporary Experience*, served as the special source of preparation for Bangkok.

The observant reader could hardly overlook the fact that the understanding of salvation presented in several of the writings in that anthology had confirmed the most extreme apprehensions of the Frankfurt Declaration. And yet the German Protestant Missionary Conference (DEMT) did not express a single objection to it. It also gave no adequate directions to its official Bangkok delegation by way of a German theological contribution to the conference. The communion in faith which used to characterize the DEMT has split asunder over the fundamental crisis of missions that is increasingly evident in all its deliberations. In his yearly report at Königsfeld the executive secretary of the DEMT, Pastor P. G. Buttler, bemoaned the tragic fact that German mission societies "are developing more and more into quarreling parties."[12] A last-minute attempt by the Bishop of Lubeck, Dr. Heinrich Meyer, D.D., a highly honored figure in the German Protestant Missions movement, to construct a united statement for the DEMT on the Bangkok theme "Salvation Today" ran aground because of resistance from speakers aligned with the radically ecumenical group.

If this was the situation among just the Germans, what could be expected from the much more pluralistic conference assembled at Bangkok? Would we in barely two weeks be able to prepare theological texts there which, first, all of us — from American fundamentalists to

---

[11] M. Schlunk, ed., *Das Wunder der Kirche unter den Völkern der Erde [The Miracle of the Church among the Peoples of the Earth]* (Stuttgart, 1939), pp. 206-208.

[12] *Das Wort in der Welt [The Word in the World]*, no. 6, 1972 (December), p. 169.

the admirers of Maoism or God-is-dead theology — could subscribe to; which, second, would truly bring light into the contemporary confusion in mission thinking;[13] and which, third, would be practical enough to give concrete direction to all the world's churches for their mission today? Would it not have been miraculous if a sudden, deep-seated inner metamorphosis had moved the 300-odd participating delegates to a single unified viewpoint? If the importance of the matters under consideration is kept in mind, the suspense with which we boarded our flight to Bangkok on 27 December, 1972, will be obvious.

[13] How wide the scope of the participants actually was is shown very dramatically by the following observation: "When one sees on the floor an activist from Central America who is interested in nothing but 'Revolution' or hears an avowed atheist from Italy who practically makes a mockery of all religious beliefs but at the time . . . is provided with ecumenical funds for several projects [cf. documents, p. 166f.], one cannot help but wonder what is coming next." M. J. Gaxiola, "Salvation Today: A Critical Report," in Ralph Winter, ed., *The Evangelical Response to Bangkok* (Pasadena, William Carey Library, 1973), p. 76.

WHAT WAS THE TASK AND SIGNIFICANCE OF BANGKOK?

2

WHAT WAS THE TASK AND SIGNIFICANCE OF BANGKOK?

I MUST CONFESS THAT the true significance of Bangkok did not fully occur to me while preparing for the conference or even at the conference itself, but only on the way home. Pinpointed exactly, my insight as presented in this book came to me during the return flight of our ecumenical party when the representative of the Protestant Press Service, Dr. F. C. Schilling, asked me this startling question in an interview: "Do you agree with the opinion that a new era of Christian mission is now beginning?"[14] At that time I was not yet aware of the statement with which the new director of the Commission on World Mission and Evangelism (CWME), Rev. Emilio Castro, had summarized the significance of the conference on its last day: "We are at the end of a missionary era and at the very beginning of the world mission."[15] It was on hearing this that I began to grasp the fact that this latest of the great World Mission Conferences, stretching back to Edinburgh in 1910, bore a truly epochal significance for the history of the ecumenical missionary movement. The final official evaluation of Bangkok was a conclusive indication of that for me.

At the conference, however, the decisive events were not so much the formal declarations, messages, and recommendations, nor even the texts of the few major speeches given there, all of which the Christians of the world will be able to read in print. For, if they are compared with what has already been said in ecumenical conferences and by individual ecumenicals, there is really nothing new. This time even Geneva does not ascribe much importance to the written conclusions, as such, according to their literal meaning — a fact indicated by the conspicuous delay in their publication. Rather, according to the first report of the Ecu-

14 German Protestant Press Service Publication, No. 8 (11 January, 1973), p. 6.
15 Ecumenical Press Service (18 January, 1973), p. 2.

menical Press Service (EPS), "the result of the meeting could not be
embodied in a theological statement or message of the kind expected
from ecumenical gatherings . . . [but it] is embodied in the lives of
those who participated and in the concrete actions of churches, missions
and ecumenical agencies which will follow from it."[16]

Other participants said later that Bangkok had not been a conference
which one could analyze by reading its documents and resolutions.
Bangkok was rather a "festival of salvation" (H. Florin), an "eschatological event" (C. F. Hallencreutz),[17] or a "happening of faith which
could not possibly be copied," as G. Hoffmann declared. The conference atmosphere was said to be characterized by the "Pentecostal-
pietistic principle."

The first desire of the meeting was, according to the official announcement, "to *celebrate* and to proclaim the kingdom of salvation." This
celebration occurred in various ways: through devotions, in silence, in
dramatic performances, by meditations, in music, art, and "happenings."
The general secretary of the Protestant Study Group for World Missions in Hamburg, Dr. Hans Florin, described the significance of these
events: "The prayers, worship services, hymns, and meetings at Bangkok are not transformable into resolutions. They are to shine through
the reports!" And the conference did in fact have this effect on many
of its participants. As a consequence, they are today spreading the news
about Bangkok with truly missionary zeal, excited by their experiences
at the conference and about its significance for churches all over the
world, yet without at the same time being able to describe with theological precision what exactly went on there. "Many local Bangkoks
must follow the first one!"[18]

Thus the essential points to grasp about Bangkok are, first, that the
participants at an ecumenical conference, acting as representatives for
their churches and missions, here took into the depths of their souls the
new view of world missions as it has been championed for years by the
leading deputies of the Commission for World Mission and Evangelism
in Geneva, and, second, that these participants, acting as "multipliers,"
are carrying this new view with them into the churches of the whole
world.

"In a sense there was a corporate conversion experience at a deeper

[16] This was the final announcement of the reflection group in Bangkok; cf.
Ecumenical Press Service (18 January, 1973), p. 7.
[17] C. F. Hallencreutz (Uppsala), "Bangkok aus eropäischer Sicht" ["Bangkok
From a European Point of View"], Ecumenical Press Service Monthly Publication
(July 1973), p. 4.
[18] H. Florin, "Bangkok 1973," mimeographed report, p. 5.

level than that of intellectual formulations," writes C. F. Hallencreutz. "The significance of the conference, however, will largely depend on how the Bangkok experience is interpreted in the life of the world Church."[19]

Immediately after Bangkok a follow-up campaign of educational instruction unlike any seen previously was begun in churches all over the world. Trusted confidants of the WCC traveled straight from Bangkok over the whole globe to spread the news about the conference. Dr. H. Florin, missions executive officer in Hamburg, for example, talked about just his own activity: "I myself have already had to report on Bangkok in Manila, Hongkong, Teheran, and Beirut!" Pastoral and theological seminars were already organized before the actual reports from the conference had appeared. This, if nothing else, shows how important Geneva considered this last World Mission Conference in the tradition of the old International Missionary Council.

At the many local Bangkoks, as even in Bangkok itself, the concern was not so much to work out and negotiate a mature understanding of missions as it was to win joyful, emotional consent for the path designated by the directing board of the WCC as the future course for world missions. Consequently, no independent biblical and theological results were expected from Bangkok; indeed the prevention of such was a conscious goal. Bangkok was instead to solidify the foundations for the action-program that has increasingly occupied the Department for World Mission and Evangelism since the integration of the International Missionary Council into the World Council of Churches. (The CWME has been a part of the "Program Unit for Faith and Witness" since the meeting of the Central Committee of the WCC in Addis Ababa in 1971.)

In order to assess the great significance of Bangkok for the history of the World Council of Churches, one must see clearly that it was the purpose of the Geneva organizers to complete the integration of the International Missionary Council into the WCC. This had first been undertaken organizationally at the New Delhi Conference in 1961; it was now also to be accomplished ideologically here at this last World Mission Conference in the outward tradition of the International Missionary Council.

To be sure, the way for this step had already been cleared at the fourth plenary session at Uppsala in 1968, especially by Section II,[20]

[19] *Loc. cit.*

[20] Cf. P. Beyerhaus, "Humanisierung — einzige Hoffnung der Welt?" ["Humanization — the Only Hope of the World?"] (Bad Salzuflen, 2nd edition, 1970).

even though the evangelical wing within the WCC had offered strong resistance. The report of Section II indicated that the central aim of the WCC — i.e., cooperation in the construction of a new world community in which all peoples, races, classes, and religions are united in peace, justice, and humanity — had now become the actual goal of the Commission for World Mission and Evangelism under the close control of the "Program Unit for Faith and Witness" of the Geneva General Secretariat.

The British Methodist, Pauline Webb, vice-chairman of the Central Committee of the WCC, succinctly summarized the goal of the ecumenical movement in the Ecumenical Press Service. In the introduction to the tasks of Bangkok, Section II ("Salvation and Social Justice"), a group which she herself chaired, she described the coming of the messianic kingdom of Christ in Marxist terms as the outgrowth of an ideologically motivated program of political liberation: "Christians have been entrusted, Dr. M. M. Thomas, chairman of the Central Committee, said in his address at Utrecht, with 'the utopian vision' and theirs is the responsibility of translating that vision into ideological reality and a practical political program of liberation for all who are oppressed."[21]

Mrs. Webb closed her article with a reference to the Marxist philosopher, Roger Garaudy, who speaks of Jesus as the One "who takes the inevitability out of history and teaches us that man is born to be the creator of his own destiny." She goes on to say: "The aim of the Section on Salvation and Social Justice will be to understand how the message of salvation in Christ does just this — takes the inevitability out of the injustice of our present national and international institutions and liberates mankind into the possibility of achieving that new order in which the kingdoms of this world indeed become the kingdoms of our God and of his Christ."[22]

Attaining the kingdom of God has thus become a human possibility, arising out of the "utopian vision" of secularized prophetic promise, inspired by Jesus' message and example, transformed into an ideology, realized through a practical program of political liberation, and guided by the World Council of Churches. Verses from the Bible, which we also studied at Bangkok, have been torn from their contexts and fixed with a Marxist ideology in order to create this thrilling syncretistic vision. Now the concern of the WCC is to have this enthusiasm catch

[21] *This Month*, No. 33, Ecumenical Press Service (December, 1972), pp. 2, 3.

[22] This quotation is from the preparatory anthology for Bangkok: *Salvation Today and Contemporary Experience* (Geneva, 1972), p. 46.

fire. Bangkok provided an important first match for this blaze which, through the efforts of ecumenical torch-bearers, is to spread like a prairie fire over the churches of the earth.

In order to gain the adherence of the WCC's constituent churches and mission agencies to this master plan and to equip them to carry it out, a threefold shift will be required in their methods and basic alignment:

(1) They have to substitute for their traditional concept of mission as bearing the message of the biblical Gospel to the non-Christian world the readiness to establish a new relationship with the adherents of other religions and ideologies ("living faiths") based on partnerships and dialogue.

(2) The concept of the uniqueness of biblical salvation, which fundamentally consists in the reconciliation of the sinner with God on the basis of the atoning death of Christ, has to give way to a much broader, essentially this-worldly concept of salvation expressed mainly in social and political categories. Only thereby would the churches and missions be prepared to join the ranks of present-day revolutionary liberation movements.

(3) The opening of the churches of the Third World for the contemporary religious and political movements in their national environment has to be secured, partly by transforming the traditional bilateral relations between mother and daughter churches into new multilateral structures, partly by cutting them entirely.

The division of the Bangkok Conference into its three sections corresponded to the three-pronged ecumenical concern: (1) Culture and Identity, (2) Salvation and Social Justice, (3) Church Renewal through Mission.

Given such a programming of the conference — so clearly obvious even in the process of preparation —, an earnest theological effort by all participants for an exegetical and doctrinal clarification of the central theme, "Salvation Today," could only function, in principle, as a brake or a destructive force. Therefore, an entirely different means had to be chosen to reach the goal: the theological study material, gathered for a period of four years, was simply allowed to disappear from sight, and in its place the delegates to Bangkok were summoned to an "experiment in group dynamics"![23] Early in December, 1972, Dr. Gerhard Hoff-

23 Cf. Dr. J. Verkuyl, *Jezus Christus, de bevrijder [Jesus Christ, the Liberator]* (The Dutch volume reporting on Bangkok), (Ten Have, 1973), chapter X, "The Application of a New Method in the Section Meetings," pp. 51, 52.

mann, the former executive secretary of the German Protestant Missionary Council who had just taken a position at the Geneva headquarters of
the CWME, sent a reply to Pastor P. G. Buttler, his successor in Hamburg. Pastor Buttler had posed a question concerning the preparatory
theological documents for Bangkok. Dr. Hoffmann responded to his
letter as follows:

> The group leaders are not tied to definite texts. They can come with
> their own preparation but they must face the insights of others who
> find other texts or interpretations more important. For the other
> groups, too, something analogous applies. [The dance group, inci-
> dentally, has been cancelled; instead the number of Bible study groups
> has been increased. HB] Preparation is not possible on a mere
> intellectual level, but rather by being tuned in to the theme. This does
> not exclude an intellectual German theological discussion, but it re-
> duces the possibility to a "contribution." As you state, the German
> delegation is crying for "preparatory material." The first answer, there-
> fore, would be: do not block yourselves against an experiment in group
> dynamics, and still less against the moving of God's Spirit, which is at
> least possible. Rather prepare yourselves in a different way this time!
> Is it not "preparation," if somebody somewhere discovers a new song,
> contemplates on it and takes it along to Bangkok? Of course he also
> may bring along biblical texts, which have just become important to
> him.

Owing to its apparent originality, this plan surprised a good number
of the delegates and encouraged them to open themselves up for the
experiment. Others, in contrast, thought it looked like the Mad Hatter's
birthday party! In the last analysis, responsibly thinking participants
felt themselves frustrated at Bangkok, particularly in theological matters.
After the first week had passed, a leading American evangelical remarked
to his friends: "This is the most boring congress I have ever participated in." He had, of course, not perceived that the boredom could be
a direct design of the guidelines governing such an experiment in group
dynamics!

The conference schedule, which was released only at the beginning
of the congress, provided space for just a very few public addresses
and still fewer opportunities to discuss them. Actually, the Geneva
establishment itself was the only voice to be heard from the podium.
Mr. M. M. Thomas, the chairman of the Central Committee, gave the
only lecture touching fundamental theological issues when he spoke
on the topic "The Meaning of Salvation." This talk was sandwiched
between two reports. One by Thomas Wieser covered the progress of
the "Salvation Today" study, and Dr. Philip Potter, as the outgoing

director of CWME, gave his general report entitled, "Christ's Mission and Ours in Today's World."[24] Next came the Bible studies under the controlling theme, "Exploring What Salvation Means. . . ." The motto of the sessions that followed was ". . . With a View to Action," and it was during this part of the schedule that the subsections and occasionally even whole sections met a total of eight times. These were actually the major events on the schedule.

The conference schedule could still have been a positive asset if the Bible studies had really laid the theological foundations for the anticipated program of ecumenical action. But the two biblical expositions offered publicly by Dr. Hans Ruedi Weber, the Geneva official in charge of Bible studies, consisted of a reader's theater production, performed by a small group, which then developed into a teaching dialogue with the full assembly. This was, to be sure, a masterful catechetical device, even if its exegetical basis was questionable. "A nice Sunday school lesson," was the telling comment of the Pakistani Bishop, Chandu Ray.

Some of the Bible-study groups, which met on three different mornings, were responsible for what I experienced as the most enjoyable feature of the conference program. In any case the demand for the Bible-study groups — these had been set up alongside other groups dealing with art, meditation, medical missions, and originally even dance for the "Exploration of Salvation" — was so strong that the four original groups had to be increased to seven. But when I inquired at the start of my group's discussion whether there would be an opportunity for us to introduce the insights gained through the study into the final results of the conference, the representatives of the World Council assigned to us explained categorically again that no formal results were expected from these groups. The groups, in effect, had been prepared for our personal edification. In relationship to the experiment in group dynamics, they functioned as introductory preparations during which we were circumspectly harmonized into the collective consciousness desired for the conference. In spite of these restrictions, two groups nevertheless prepared formal statements and published them on the bulletin boards and in the conference newspaper. One finally succeeded, supplemented by ecumenical emendations, in finding a place in the final report of the plenary assembly under the title "An Affirmation on Salvation Today."[25]

The major assignment, that of preparing the recommendations that

24 Excerpts from these addresses are found in the documentary section, 4.
25 See the documentary section: 6, B.

were to be the *raison d'être* of the conference, was given, at least nominally, to the ten subsections into which the three main sections were divided. But even they were not able to draw up any truly unified reports that were responsibly and theologically grounded. It was not even intended that they should do so. Rather, the first conference from 29 December 1972, to 8 January, 1973, was supposed to set in motion the spiritual impetus which would enable the General Assembly of the CWME, meeting from 9 to 12 January, 1973, to take the concrete actions expected from the churches.[26]

Manuel J. Gaxiola, president of the Church of Apostolic Faith in Mexico, wrote this about the relationship of the Salvation Today Conference to the General Assembly which followed it:

> We cannot, however, deny that there were in each and every group a few people who clearly sought to get across what seems to be the main preoccupation of the WCC . . . to involve the Church in social, political, and economical concerns which cannot be but secondary. . . . Many people felt the resolutions to be taken after many of the participants had left were actually "prefabricated" and would in no way reflect the biblical insights that had been gained in the Bible study groups.[27]

Hans Florin expressed it like this:

> The General Assembly following the conference once again took up all the themes and developed them where possible into recommendations and resolutions for the churches. That this was not always so easy can well be imagined. The General Assembly did its business by the committee system which was most familiar to us. In and with these limitations, the Spirit, the dynamic, the challenge of Bangkok were to be poured into those forms which alone still seem binding on us for our activity. This comment implies that the ecumenical idea is that the spirit of a world conference, as engineered by the group dynamic method should drive the member churches directly into the desired actions without the medium of printed resolutions. Because then no debate of principle will be possible any more due to the lack of documental evidence.[28]

---

[26] The official schedule of the "Salvation Today" conference said on p. 17: "The practical steps proposed by the subsections will not be formally voted on but will be addressed directly to the bodies most competent to act, including . . . the CWME Assembly following the conference."

[27] *Op. cit.*, p. 62.

[28] H. Florin, "Bangkok 1973," mimeographed report, p. 5.

HOW WAS THE SALVATION QUESTION
ANSWERED AT BANGKOK?

3

HOW WAS THE SALVATION QUESTION
ANSWERED AT BANGKOK?

OUR THIRD GUIDING question consciously addresses the manner in which the congress was conducted before discussing in the next chapter the results of the congress.

Even a first, dispassionate reading of some of the Bangkok findings and resolutions as reported by the press took the breath away from non-participants. The call for a temporary suspension (or moratorium) on the sending of further missionaries, and the China Resolution were particularly shocking.[29] The burning question arises immediately: How could these recommendations and resolutions have been composed without the presence of any dissent or even a minority opinion both in the conference made up of 326 delegates considering the theme "Salvation Today" and in the smaller General Assembly of the CWME following it and sitting from 9 to 12 January, 1973, when both groups were so thoroughly divided? My impressions at Bangkok lead me to find the answer in the method practiced there and the atmosphere fostered by it. In this, perhaps for the first time in my life, I am in complete agreement with one of the leading ecumenical officials who played a very important role in the planning and execution of the Bangkok Conference: Dr. Walter Hollenweger, the former Swiss Pentecostal evangelist and, later, secretary for evangelism of the WCC in Geneva who is now employed as a professor of missions in Birmingham.

Hollenweger was interviewed in Bangkok not only by the Second German Television but also by Southwest German Radio. In these interviews he stated that the most important aspect of the entire conference for him was its new method which was being practiced there for the first time at an ecumenical World Conference.

What actually was this method? In the letter cited above from Geneva to Hamburg, Hollenweger's successor, Dr. Gerhard Hoffmann, called the method planned for Bangkok an experiment in group dynam-

29 See the documentary section: 8, B, C.

ics. Such experiments seek to create a specific psychological climate within a group composed of all sorts of people; in this group all the participants, in spite of their original resistance, are finally brought into a united community of emotions, thought, and will. The Geneva officials, who desired this mass psychological movement, sought to relate it to the "movement of the Spirit of God"!

The true key to understanding the planning and the course of the Bangkok Conference lies in this professed equation of a systematically staged, socio-psychological experiment with the action of the Holy Spirit. If someone wants to understand aright the individual components of the Bangkok program, the conduct of the organizers, the reaction of the participants, and the final results, he must busy himself not only with the forms of extremist Pentecostal movements but also with the subject of group dynamics as it has been developed in America and, to a certain extent, in England since the Second World War. Of special importance to the latter subject is one of its two main branches, namely Sensitivity Training. It was first developed through a discovery made by the important American social psychologist, Kurt Lewin, as he was guiding an experimental course in group dynamics at New Britain Teacher's College in August, 1946.[30] From these small experimental beginnings arose, first, a new branch of social scientific investigation and then a popular movement with diverse practical applications and also world-wide expansion. There is, particularly in the United States, a wealth of workshops, laboratories, educational schemes, books, and tapes in which the methods of Sensitivity Training are more thoroughly developed and which have been placed at the disposal of those interested in it: scientists, industrial managers, educators, psychotherapists, politicians, private persons thirsting for experience, and now even ecclesiastical, particularly ecumenical, officials.

Kurt Back has said of this movement: "Some enthusiasts of sensitivity training have compared its impact with that of the discovery of atomic energy, asserting that atomic energy gave us a great amount of physical power to control the physical universe, and sensitivity training gave us the power to control the personal universe."[31]

Sensitivity Training has two critically essential features: it gives its participants a tremendous emotional experience that they can even sometimes describe as a new birth. And it is considered, and also

[30] The most important scholarly introduction into the source and development of Sensitivity Training is provided by Kurt W. Back, *Beyond Words: The Story of Sensitivity Training and the Encounter Movement* (New York, 1972).

[31] *Ibid.*, p. 14.

praised, by its advocates as an invaluable means to alter people inwardly and, thereby, to make them better members of their group and better listeners to it; in so doing it is even said to equip them properly for the changed realities of our modern world.

There are any number of Sensitivity Training centers; these can be regarded almost as modern counterparts to the pilgrim shrines of earlier days that drew religious men thirsting for salvation. In the United States the National Training Laboratory heads the list of these places as a model research and educational center. The vocabulary used by Hollenweger and Hoffmann to describe the group dynamics experiment, that is, the method used at Bangkok, reveals to initiates that they are experts in Sensitivity Training. And the same could also be said about all the organizers primarily responsible for the conference on the basis of their behavior there.

Sensitivity Training is a new movement in which, according to Kurt Back, "ideology, pragmatism, opportunism, transcendence, and scientific method" have entered into "a singular alliance." Of particular note in this is "that sensitivity training has had religious undertones since its beginning. In its drifting away from strictly scientific procedures it has assumed the religious function of providing a consistent world view and some of the emotional aspects and controls of religious ritual. It has tended to become a religiously oriented social movement."[32]

The congress at the remote conference center, twenty miles outside of Bangkok, was to provide a first, but critical, encounter with this movement, even if for the majority of the delegates it was completely unexpected. Even we West German participants were not instructed in the particulars of what was to be expected from such an "experiment in group dynamics." But we soon found out for certain.

Critically important for the success of such an experiment is, in Hoffmann's words, the complete mutual "openness" of the participants to the expressions of each other, or, as Hollenweger put it, their inner "vulnerability." These are his words in the Southwest German Radio interview:

> The most important aspect of the conference for me is the method, illustrated by the fact that the preparatory volume is made up of short excerpts, poems, song lyrics, and Chanson texts from all over the world. I know of no conference, ecclesiastical or otherwise, that has put so much material from non-European cultures directly into its preliminary documents. In the groups, similarly, a great deal of stress will be placed on the *interaction* of the participants, even on their talk-

[32] *Ibid.*, p. 19.

ing to each other. This will not only be discussion on an academic plane, but the kind of discussion which touches the heart of men. We hope that there are enough people here who are *vulnerable* and who will let themselves be *wounded* so that they can hear the *strange* things and the *unheard of* things and the things which have *never yet been heard* that others will say to them.

This meant that we should be ready to call all the convictions and presuppositions that we brought with us into question, and even that we should abandon them under certain conditions in order to open ourselves up to the "unheard of thing," perhaps even that which contradicts our understanding of the Christian faith. "Vulnerability" essentially entails an emotional sensitivity, particularly in the area of the conscience for Christians, so that one can take up the needs of another or confess his guilt for causing their distresses.

The conference wanted to involve its participants in the ecumenical socio-political movement. But for the success of a new social movement, four fundamental factors are important, according to the American sociologist H. Blumer.[33] First, a general *uneasiness* in which men are responsive to a new appeal; second, a popular *rising* in which all are agreed as to the sources of the difficulty and in which the goals of the movement are clearly defined; third, *indoctrination*, that is, the creation of a body of dogmas and a vanguard of adherents to disseminate them; and fourth, *institutionalization* which is necessary in order to realize the goals of the movement.

In this process the steps taken for indoctrination are particularly crucial. Sensitivity Training does not indoctrinate by theoretical concepts presented in informative addresses and lectures. Rather, indoctrination proceeds directly at the level of human emotions. Such indoctrination can be carried out in any number of ways by the "interaction" of participants in group discussions and "happenings," through audio-visual aids, or by mystical and ritualistic devotional exercises. The success of the method depends upon the inclusion of enough people in a group, though not too many to be controlled, who in moving fashion talk about their personal needs. All the discussions, audio-visual aids, songs, and even prayers must be concerned with these personal needs while all other topics and "unstructured influences" are to be excluded. If the method succeeds, a new ideological consciousness is communicated to the group by interpreting all personal difficulties with a very specific, constantly repeated vocabulary of code words like

---

[33] H. Blumer, "Collective Behavior," in A. M. Lee, ed., *Principles of Sociology* (New York, 1951), pp. 165-222.

"dehumanization, loss of identity, powerlessness" and by turning out a scapegoat responsible for these personal troubles. The participants appropriate this new ideological consciousness emotionally as a "spontaneous discovery," and they — at least at first — are also ready to take part in actions suited to this new consciousness in the future.

In Bangkok, as a matter of fact, there was a great deal of talk about contemporary needs and about guilt.

But there was practically no discussion of the needs of a guilty conscience before the wrath of God; the guilt which we all share alike before God — also fellow Christians of other races — was a subject left in the fringes of discussion. There was almost no mention of *that* need and *that* guilt which oppressed and oppressing men suffer and cause on the other side of the Iron Curtain in Russia and China. Much talk at Bangkok referred to the crucified Christ. But the cross was almost never interpreted as a sin offering necessitated by the guilt of sinners of all races before God. Rather it was almost always understood as the suffering shared by Jesus, or God, with the poor and oppressed of the Third World. It had this sense even in the "Letter to the Churches": "The cross of Christ where his love went to the bitter end forces us to recognize how often we stop along the road and impells us to start walking joyously even if the path leads to sacrifice."

We white participants were in the minority at Bangkok, and we were for all intents and purposes in the dock right from the start. We were indicted by the colored church leaders, by adherents of the Black Power Movement, and by Viet Cong sympathizers from South Vietnam. In an early official Ecumenical Press Service report from Bangkok it was said: "The triumph of the conference is the relentless declarations of the Third World." And in the conference newspaper, *Yesterday*, one could read on page two of the January 7 issue: "Someone has called this a 'sado-masochistic duel' with one side hurling those recriminations and the other accepting them in toto either by their silence on the floor or by a grudging acceptance when talking in private or in small groups."

Walter Gengnagel, the leader of the German branch of the Basel Mission, described this experience in an address in Balingen on 14 April, 1973. His description is penetrating and at the same time instructive:

> One particular afternoon session sticks in my memory with special force. One African after another told of experiencing bitter political oppression and economic exploitation. The established churches and missions, it was said, must share the responsibility for this oppression. They were silent for too long about injustice or in many cases even participated themselves in it. The representatives of the Third World

expressed their open displeasure even with well-intentioned attempts to help. In even these efforts the West had forced them to accept its own programs, its own ideas. "We are not the raw material with which others can work out their salvation," said one African. The atmosphere in the conference hall was tense. The Europeans, confounded, were silent. Justifications and excuses culled from the historical study of missions did not seem to fit the occasion. We sensed at once with too much clarity the rightful basis of the complaints. We realized with too much intensity that *wounded* [compare Hollenweger! PB] men were standing before us here and talking to us. At that moment Philip Potter took the floor: "We can now only appeal for help to that One who is the only One able to help us in this situation." And with that the more than 300 delegates from 69 countries spontaneously uttered those lines which had become a kind of theme for us at the conference: "Out of the depths I cry unto Thee, O Lord!"

A similar report was given by H. J. Girock on Southwest German Radio, Baden-Baden: "At various times startled silence reigned among the western delegates, and when one of them did take the floor, it was rare when he did not begin with a specific confession of guilt for the mistakes of the past."

One certainly wonders at the alarming resemblance between this one-sided process of political charges and self-accusation and the Chinese show trials or other "peoples' courts" that are used by totalitarian regimes for massive indoctrination, a process also known as "brainwashing."[34]

As a last analysis of this phenomenon we will quote a comment by Dr. John V. Taylor, the general secretary of the largest British missionary agency, the Anglican Church Missionary Society:

> At times it seemed that all the 55% [the delegates from the Third World identified the white delegates with exploitation and oppression.

[34] That this is no slander of Sensitivity Training is clearly seen from the following, highly official definition which was provided in the handbook for group leaders, *In Training*, published by the *National Training Laboratories* in 1962 (p. 47): "Sensitivity training is defined as group meetings, large or small, to discuss publicly intimate and personal matters, and opinions, values or beliefs; and/or, to act out emotions and feelings toward one another in the group, using the techniques of self-confession and mutual criticism. It is also 'coercive persuasion in the form of thought reform or brain-washing!'" The use of this concept in an ecumenical conference is certainly shocking. It is however pointed out that American social-psychology can also speak of "brainwashing" in an educational sense and can shape certain methods according to this principle. The article by Prof. R. F. Creegan of the State University of New York ("'Brainwash': Some Wider Implications," *School and Society*, 84 [1956]: 140, 141) was important for me in understanding the Bangkok Conference.

At this point the theology, which quite rightly includes political and economic liberation in the full meaning of salvation, begins to take on an ideological tone of voice which is ugly and partisan. We were treated to a good deal of the selective indignation which, in my view, has marred the social witness of the World Council of Churches in recent years. . . . Condemnation would be far more credible if it were directed impartially against every gross transgression of human rights.

In some ways this was not the best atmosphere in which to discuss the relationship between missionary agencies and the churches of the Third World. It is a little harder to agree that "we are at the end of a missionary era" when this was made to sound like "Death to the imperialists!"[35]

Whether all representatives of the Third World were actually so hostile to the missionaries from Europe is of course doubtful. There also existed a silent majority which hardly even announced a desire to speak, but which had quiet questions about much that was seen and heard in Bangkok. One of their number, the elderly black Bishop S. U. Hastings of the Moravian Brethren from Kingston in Jamaica, took the floor in the last plenary session to insert a word of vindication for the sake of fairness to the white missionaries:

I come from a completely independent church. Our discussion of missions has had no balance. Up to this point we have spoken too negatively of missions. I want to say something positive. The old missionaries gave what they had. It is not right to judge the missionaries of the eighteenth century by the standards of the twentieth. The missionaries did much to abolish slavery and to procure land for those who had none. They brought education and the light of salvation. We would not be able to talk about "Salvation Today" if missionaries had not brought us salvation. My country belongs to the Third World. The missionaries gave us the tools by which we can stand up for freedom today. Let there be light, the darkness has reigned long enough.

In spite of all that had been said in the earlier sessions, his words were greeted by surprisingly strong applause, even from the rows of the Afro-Asian delegations!

But Bishop Hastings' voice was the only one that was raised in opposition to the general trend. It was not representative of the attitude taken toward missions by official leaders, especially by the chief representatives of the All-African Church Conference which had been invited to Bangkok by the Geneva headquarters.

[35] J. V. Taylor, "Bangkok and After," in Church Missionary Society newsletter, No. 370 (April 1973), p. 5.

Even the impressive opening address by General Secretary Philip Potter was a biting settlement of historical accounts with western missions, its entanglement in colonialism and imperialism, and its failure to minister to the social and political needs of the African and Asian peoples. And later we were indicted time after time for our failure to act in the Vietnam question and for our participation in white racism. Our patronizing attitude as western churches and missions in relation to the churches of the Third World was also condemned. We have, it was said, gagged the Third World churches spiritually and kept them from finding their "true identity," that is, religious, cultural, and social self-reliance.

The concept of power appeared time and again as a means of describing our greatest sin and at the same time as a means of providing the key to answering the salvation question. A new distribution of power from the western churches to the indigenous churches would allow a true experience of salvation to take place today. "If one is looking for an encompassing catchword, 'power' strikes me as appropriate," Gerhard Hoffmann said in his report on the Bangkok Conference.[36] Of course, the use of this concept did not arise spontaneously. Rather, Philip Potter had introduced this key idea in his opening remarks, and Gerhard Hoffmann, as secretary of Section I, took pains to point out to the three subsections of Section I that the question of power was their common problem.[37]

The actual locus of this power was thought to be in the money possessed by the western missionary societies, a power which was further aligned with western capitalism. Rev. Herbert Daughtry, a preacher in a black Pentecostal congregation in Brooklyn and also one of the most radical advocates of the Black Power Movement, quoted from Potter's report that 60% of the missionaries come from the United States, 40% from Western Europe and Australia: "All are paid out of the revenues amassed by exploiting societies. How can a church be a church if it is dependent upon such resources? Isn't it true that even the church needs liberation (salvation)?"

The concept of power was also frequently reversed, so that people talked about the "power of the powerless" or even demanded a "theology of powerlessness." This could probably be identified with what Potter in another connection called the "death wish": "We have to be willing to die so that renewal and new life may come." In the same

[36] Cf. Protestant Press Service Documents (26 March, 1973), p. 42.

[37] A. H. van den Heuvel in J. Verkuyl, ed., *Jezus Christus, de bevrijder [Jesus Christ, the Liberator]*, chapter XI, p. 54.

place he expresses the idea in yet another way: "For the sake of our concern for human rights we should have a few screws loose. . . . We must be daring, we must be fools for Christ. Sanity is the death of the ecumenical movement."[38] (At this particular point I am inclined to agree with the General Secretary of the World Council of Churches.)

The Geneva organizers of the conference and their ecumenical colleagues spared themselves no pains in the effort to communicate as forcibly as possible their vision of "lostness" and salvation to the delegates. G. Hoffmann explained in this regard: "Through the method used at the conference, group processes were set in motion which compelled the individual participants to speak and listen existentially, and in this atmosphere of interpersonal encounter all efforts to construct abstract and systematic theology seemed almost inhuman, and certainly non-Christian."[39] It is thus proper to refer explicitly to a realized exercise of Sensitivity Training at Bangkok. A whole series of resources existed to implement this. First and foremost among these were the loyal consultants supported financially by Geneva; they made up perhaps one-third of all who participated. A substantial number of these consultants made the most of the accuser's role that has been described; others helped to guide the discussions along lines designed to move human feelings.

A part of the strategy for the conference was to hold only a few plenary sessions, just eight for eleven days, in order to have more meetings in small groups. In these groups we were to testify of our experiences of salvation or distress. Hoffmann has called Bangkok "a kind of pietistic testimony meeting" — with, of course, testimonies expressing a predetermined socio-political point of view being the ones desired here. I experienced this selectivity myself in Subsection I B when a young, evangelical Christian from West Africa movingly related his own conversion from Islam to Christ. This testimony was passed over without further comment or evaluation. Much greater significance was apportioned to the story of a Chinese intellectual who had been reduced to working in a pig pen during the Cultural Revolution. In this experience he discovered that he needed a "conversion" in order to accept the simple peasant as his fellowman. The final report of Section I went so far as to include this kind of biographical material.

Although these small groups were designed to give every conference participant the opportunity to express himself personally, the discussions were nevertheless under the imperceptible, but secure control of their

[38] Religious News Service (2 May, 1973), p. 18.
[39] Protestant Press Service Documents (26 March, 1973), p. 42.

leaders; and they knew where they wanted to go. Helping the leaders was a novel class of assistants who in Bangkok were known by the unusual title of "reflectors." They maintained the connection with the conference leadership at the so-called reflection sessions, but time and again they also contributed sensitizing input to the discussions in such a way as to lead them in the desired direction. This sort of worker in Sensitivity Training is also called an "animator" or "agent of change" in other contexts. But of course their function was not disclosed to the majority of the participants who had not yet had experience in Sensitivity Training.

Back describes the role of the Sensitivity Trainer as follows:

> The trainer has a responsibility that goes beyond expert knowledge, to use the action of the group to fulfill the purposes of the training. Although his role might be quite passive, he has to know when he must intervene to keep the group within the experience that sensitivity training is supposed to provide. The trainer, therefore, has the responsibility to set limits on the activities of the group, so that it does not get too emotional and does not try to escape from the present situation by discussing some outside problem. He must push toward the correct interpretations and, in general, keep the group going. . . . The illusion of democracy in a group of this kind is equivalent to the illusion that the trainer really relinquishes his role. A good trainer makes the group feel that he comes out of the group, but at the same time he leads it toward the relevant experiences and provides the relevant indoctrination. . . .[40]

It cannot be said that all "reflectors" in Bangkok were completely up to their task, since particularly at this point the coordination which had been planned often went awry. And of course not all the ecumenical trustees actually functioning as "trainers" had official positions as group leaders or reflectors.

Only later, after further consideration, did I grasp clearly the importance of the individual proceedings for the unified work of the conference.

The import of the Bangkok section reports is actually only fully revealed when some acquaintance has been gained with the ideological forms of Sensitivity Training, especially as they have been developed in the United States in special experimental institutions. The Ecumenical Institute of Chicago deserves special mention in this regard; it has recently begun to spread its influence over all the world through a network of daughter institutions. Pains are taken to give indigenous

---

[40] Back, *op. cit.*, p. 106.

church workers intensive courses of instruction, taught by directors trained in this technique, in order to put the churches on a new course. The important thing to note is the new interpretation of Christian talk that is undergirded by an ideology mediated through group dynamics. As "renewed churches" they are then supposed to be able to contribute their share to the renewal of this world.[41]

A strikingly scintillating rhetoric is used throughout almost the entire report from Section I at Bangkok, "Culture and Identity." But it is a rhetoric that shies away from clear theological statements. Almost all the texts can be read in a Christian or theological sense, an ideological sense, or even a general religious sense — and all with equal support from the documents themselves. Many of the concepts here are expressed in the typical code words of the new ideology developed by American sensitivity programs: humanity, identity, liberation, sensibility, creativity, interaction, communication, frustration, etc. But even biblical words like salvation, hope, faith, conversion, praise, prayer, and litany have also taken on an indiscriminately religious or humanitarian tone.[42] This did not happen by chance, for the central concern of Section I was the relationship of Christianity to other religions and ideologies. In fact, interreligious dialogue was demonstrated publicly in a Buddhist monastery near Bangkok by the first subsection, I A, "On Dialogue With People of Living Faiths."

These reports — which to a large extent are made up of meditations, novel forms of prayer, litanies, and acclamations — sketch the blurred contours of an approaching unified religion in which Christianity contributes merely some formal suggestions for the general ideas of God and salvation. Inasmuch as the name of Christ, in the sense of the cosmic Christology promulgated at New Delhi, is still retained, this is a typical, alluring example of syncretism, even if Gerhard Hoffmann has tried to negate this criticism by the categorical declaration: "The spectre of a panreligious syncretism did not appear once on the horizon at Bangkok." Yet this was, nevertheless, the first Christian conference in the history of the Church to be opened by a message from the head of a non-Christian world religion, Princess Poon Pismai Diskul, president of the World Fellowship of Buddhists. Her message was read to us by the general secretary of the Buddhist World Fellowship, Aiem Sangkhavasi. It closed with these words: "May I invoke the Grace of

41 Cf. P. Beyerhaus, *In Ostasien erlebt [Experiences in East Asia]* (Stuttgart, 1972), p. 119.

42 Cf. the collation of such ideologically reinterpreted biblical concepts in modern ecumenical rhetoric in the attached documents: 6, appendix.

whatever is sacred and divine in the universe: . . . the Triple Gem, the Holy Trinity, or others, to give us their blessings for our success in the task we are undertaking for other people . . . and happiness and peace and security, and most important of all, *Salvation.*"

Here is a syncretistic prayer right in the opening ceremonies![43] And yet Hoffmann once again assured us about this matter at the conclusion of his address by trying to make the objections of those who assess things differently seem ridiculous: "The age-old European, theological phantom of a frenzied syncretism destroying all boundaries (our boundaries of course, not God's boundaries!) did not even appear once on the horizon. Whoever claims to have seen it in Bangkok must have brought it along in the suitcase of his own psychological inhibitions."

Only a person who has purposefully unlearned the capacity to make conceptually definite statements in order to open the gates to ecumenical religious enthusiasm can defend the texts under consideration with a good conscience. It matters little that, since the Apostle Paul, clear, unambiguous assertions have been essential to Christian theology, and not only western theology. But this too is characteristic of Sensitivity Training, as in this case theological argument about facts is replaced by a self-styled psychotherapeutic diagnosis. If the exercise in Sensitivity Training should fail for a participant and he remain spiritually independent, thus becoming a so-called "blocker," he is considered an unteachable discussion partner and simply declared to be neurotic!

In any case, if one considers the polished poetic form of the documents in Section I, it is obvious that there is no way in which they could be the joint conclusions of a group discussion. To the contrary, they have been written by poetically gifted individuals who extracted from the discussions the very ideas which they themselves had introduced as a part of the sensitivity program. Unanimous agreement by

---

[43] There was no Christian prayer in this opening ceremony, certainly out of consideration for the feelings of the Buddhist groups. But Buddhist and other Eastern religious elements certainly did find their way into the devotional life of a few participants, particularly those who chose for their "Exploration of the Meaning of Salvation" the group "Contemplation" under the leadership of the Anglican Father Murray Rogers (now of Jerusalem, formerly of India). Church president Manuel J. Gaxiola was originally in this group. "But after one session at Father Rogers' group, he [Gaxiola] decided he would not return the next day, for what was actually happening there . . . was . . . rather a mixture of practices, Christian and non-Christian, which could be classified as a syncretistic cult. A ceremony was conducted which was actually a Buddhist ceremony, with all the paraphernalia that go with it and, of course, with certain Christian elements which were relegated to second place." Gaxiola, *op. cit.*, p. 70.

the groups to the documents, which had in effect been prepared ahead of time, was obtained through the use of some such trusty formula as: "I believe the consensus of our group can be summarized like this . . ." — and that, even if participants had expressed completely antithetical views on the question during discussion!

The success of such a plan depends on the ability to isolate contrary participants, recognized in the discussion as "blockers," directing the displeasure of the group upon them, and as much as possible keeping them from speaking. The chairmen of the subsections were also careful, quite consciously, not to raise the question of the written report to be drawn up from the discussion too early, "for that would certainly hinder a free exchange of opinions." Instead they often allowed the discussions to go so far overtime that there would be no time left at the end to jointly prepare the section report. In most such cases the assignment to compose the report fell almost automatically to the editorial committee provided by the conference leadership or to the individual discussion leader himself. It was my firsthand experience, for example, in Subsection I B, "Cultural Identity and Conversion," that in its sixth of eight sessions we could not agree whether Christian conversion was something unique by comparison with conversion experiences in Maoism or other religions — and the report of this discussion was ultimately written by the concerned ecumenical chairman himself!

One particularly informative text is the one that concludes the segment of meditations in the report of Section I. Although it bore the title "An Affirmation of Faith," it was actually a description in semi-theological terms of the experience of a typical session in Sensitivity Training. It was also reproduced by Gerhard Hoffmann in his Bangkok report, "because it provides a lively image of the methods used at this conference."[44] This is how it began:

> We came from almost too many situations, with the usual prejudice, our own ideas, our exaggerated hopes, many of us tired of conferences, all of us full of our own preoccupations.
>
> Then we shared our biographical materials, struggling to express our thoughts, groping for words that might communicate, hurting each other by hasty reactions, being hurt when not heard, showing some of the frustrations we have in our work back home, sharing our fear for the future of the world, our feeble faith.
>
> And in that process we were met by God Himself, who revealed Himself in His Word, which we studied, in our friends around the table who questioned us, who gave us new insights, comforted us,

[44] Protestant Press Service Documents (28 March, 1973), p. 46.

accepted our limitations. [The last "who" is ambiguous, probably consciously, with reference to either "friends" or "God".]

This is a model description of a "self-experiencing group," as Sensitivity Training is also called sometimes: a group of people, all strangers to each other at first, encounter one another in a circle, each member occupied with his own problems and preoccupied with his own concerns. Then gradually they begin to open themselves to each other, to express thoughts and feelings freely. In the process they do not even refrain from threatening each other aggressively and wounding each other. But finally when they release the emotions and aggressions that have been dammed up, they feel relieved, understood, and accepted by the others who have revealed themselves to be just as weak and needy as themselves. It is a kind of secularized, depth-psychological absolution that takes the place of the forgiveness of sins and in fact is even identified as reconciliation with God — yet in this process the reconciling work of Christ plays no role. Christ's work is not even mentioned in this "Affirmation of Faith" which closes with the following sentences:

Not more than a glimpse of God we saw,
a smile of his grace,
a gentle gesture of judgment.

And so we repented, because we saw that God is so much greater than we.

We experienced the meek force of God's invitation to continuous conversion:

and we accepted to be sent back whence we came,
a little better motivated, a little wiser, a little sadder,
a little closer to Him.

In connection with this aspect of Sensitivity Training, Back's reference to the poet Heinrich Heine is helpful. Heine is reported to have said calmly on his deathbed: "God will forgive me, that's His job." Back goes on:

This is the kind of relationship that exists between each member of the encounter group and the audience. . . . At some point there is a strong expression of emotion caused by a really deep, intensive experience which does not last, but whose memory gives the impression that something very important happened. Despite all the aggression demonstrated during the session, or maybe because of it, there is a warm feeling which is remembered as the main flavor of the experience.[45]

Other Bangkok participants of course contest this interpretation of the World Conference as a large-scale exercise in Sensitivity Training.

[45] Back., *op. cit.*, pp. 139; 138.

Yet the Geneva organizers themselves point expressly to the group dynamics process as creating the actual mood intended for the Bangkok gathering. By virtue of their failure to see this, however, the participants did not succed in gathering their own diverse impressions of Bangkok into an intelligible whole. Walter Gengnagel, for example, called my criticism — that Bangkok was an exercise in manipulation by group dynamics — "simply absurd." In refuting my contention he was content to argue that "a conference of 300 articulate church leaders and missionaries is hardly manipulable without more going on." But Gengnagel is wrong. It is even possible to use masses of people, as both communism and National Socialism have proven. I doubt, however, if Pastor Gengnagel is really so naive about this matter, for his own mission society has for years given compulsory courses in Sensitivity Training to its missionary candidates at its institute in Basel.

Dr. F. Künneth, who occupied a leading position on the Geneva staff from 1966 to 1970, has reported that he received his first impulses toward Sensitivity Training as early as 1967 at an ecumenical conference in Nairobi.

There are others, now, who think that it is a good thing for Sensitivity Training to be introduced into many phases of the established German churches, as for example at the Protestant Academies. I do not think that this evaluation is justified. For Sensitivity Training always leads to a change in the personality. Like the so-called charismatic renewal, it makes people weak in their characters and spirits, unable to resist dangerous influences, by destroying the protective layers of normal social behavior. By these unprincipled means many people in different places have been programmed into accepting the common morality, the common world view, and the ideological code words of a particular group.[46] Such "sensitized" people have lost the individual ty which God has given to them. As a consequence, such people will let themselves be swept along by any movement capturing the loyalty of their group; they are the ones who will go along willingly should a Führer, gifted with demonic charisma, establish himself as the dictator of a society prepared by such training. There can be no doubt, in any case, that such a questionable method deserves condemnation when it is practiced in a gathering where the majority does not even have the faintest ideas about its working precepts. But this, in my opinion, is exactly what we experienced at Bangkok.

I am also convinced that the choice of a conference center as remote

---

[46] Cf. E. Smit, *De gevaren van sensitivity training [The Awareness of Sensitivity Training]* (Amsterdam, 1972), pp. 5ff.

and as difficult to reach as the Red Cross center, Samut Prakan, lying twenty miles outside of the city, was quite deliberate. This intensely planned operation in group dynamics was, to the extent possible, not to be interrupted by excursions of the participants nor disturbed by extraneous influences from the outside. Other recent ecumenical conferences of this type have also been held in similar out-of-the-way places. Even the exchange of news with the outside world was beset with almost insuperable difficulties. One participant complained: "Dr. Potter tells us that the news of the world can be heard in every land and can be seen on the television screen while it is happening. Was he trying to disprove his point by bringing us to a Conference Center where the news is rumor, where a phone call to Bangkok is an achievement?"[47]

The actual reporting of the conference was also narrowly confined by the structure of the conference. The journalists, like the other participants, had to select for themselves one of the many groups as their special area for the whole conference; they were also not permitted to quote from discussions carried on in these groups. The press conferences were given by members of the staff and dealt with themes which they themselves had selected. They thus were used to spread world-wide the official ecumenical interpretation of the questions treated at Bangkok, as for example, Dialogue, China, Partnership, and so forth.

The daily conference newspaper, Salvation Today, also called Yesterday, edited by Walter Hollenweger, was an important part of the group dynamics apparatus. In it we could air our grievances and express our approval about topics of concern. Even disputes among ourselves served in fact to set the group dynamics process in motion and help create a common conference atmosphere which could bind us together even in our differences. A similar purpose was served by the large caricatures of a young Japanese artist, Yushi Nomura, which severely chas-

---

[47] The conference newspaper, Salvation Today, no. 5 (4 January, 1973), p. 2. R. F. Creegan has written in the article we have already mentioned (fn. 34), p. 140: "Research . . . seems to indicate that the average human being will lose temporarily his power of reasoning if he is largely cut off from external stimuli for several hours. . . . Then any so-called information which is 'fed in' will tend to become incorporated into the system of beliefs. . . . The extremely comfortable environments which have been prescribed for counseling sessions, human relations conferences, educational retreats, and the like almost completely isolate individuals from certain stimuli to critical thought. It is not always easy to draw the line between that isolation which liberates the thinking process from irrelevant distractions and that isolation which deprives it of valuable or perhaps indispensable supports. The same difficulty exists whether we are concerned with individual thought or with group or conference methods."

tened the indifferent reactions of the conference participants to the many needs of our time.

At the same time, sensitizing exercises somewhat in the style of the Cologne "Political Night Prayers" filled the midday devotions. These brought us face to face with the sufferings of Africa (by the theme, "Unity in Disunity"[48]) or Vietnam through protest songs, information, and political accusations masquerading as prayers ("Out of the depth I cry unto Thee, O Lord!"). At the African devotions the representative of the Jesus People uttered this typically suggesive prayer of thanks at the beginning of the prayer service: "O God, we thank You that we are now beginning to feel the movement of Your Spirit coming down upon us!" At the end of the service the participants formed a physical chain by joining hands or embracing and then sang "Peace from the Prince of Peace." Not all participants felt easy under this approach. Nita Barrow, a West Indian official in Geneva, had this to say of the service: "During the 'kiss of peace' some people were afraid that they might be kissed. Cultural background inhibited them. Before you can get them kissing you have to warm them up with a few good revival hymns."[49]

I personally felt a different kind of inhibition regarding this form of the peace greeting. I had already encountered this rite of forming all participants into a chain through mutual touching at the rallies of other enthusiastic groups. The effect clearly resembled a closed electric circuit which transmits the energies of a few participants to the others and diffuses a singularly ecstatic atmosphere. G. Hoffmann has also spoken of the *Pentecostal-pietistic mood of the conference* in his report. Physicists know that every person has a specific electric charge and that it can be passed on by touch or even emanation. This is the operative principle of enthusiastic religion as well as spiritualism and telepathy, in terms of their psycho-physical foundations. Such an activity leaves people especially receptive for spiritual impulses from other people.

Many of the Bangkok participants have stressed the fact that this was a particularly "devout" conference in contrast with many earlier conferences.[50] They point, on the one hand, to the central place given to the Bible study groups in three full mornings at the beginning of the

[48] See the documentary section: 3.

[49] Conference newspaper, *Yesterday* (1 January, 1973), p. 4.

[50] Michael Mildenberger has written in his report, "Heil heute" ["Salvation Today"], distributed by the Protestant Coordinating Office for World View Questions [Evangelische Zentralstelle fur Weltanschauungsfragen], Stuttgart (April, 1973), p. 1: "In reality, for example, there has never yet been such a biblically oriented and in the best sense of the word 'devout' ecumenical conference."

conference. Although these seven groups were manifestly varied, I can confirm that I was pleased with my own group, under the chairmanship of the Greek bishop, Anastasios Yanoulatos. Most of us seemed to adhere to a theology quite loyal to the norms of Scripture and the confessions — above all the Lutheran and Orthodox confessions. And the efforts of our "reflector" to sensitize the group were rebuffed by our theological resistance. The most regrettable thing, as has been noted, was that we could not insert the fruits of our Bible study into the conclusions of the conference.

When, on the other hand, people point to the midday devotions as an evidence of the heightened spiritual character of the conference, I must register a radically dissenting opinion. Without doubt these too fit in with the religious atmosphere stressed at the conference. This fact had struck the journalists, who remembered well the ecumenical secularizing theology which was still flowering in Uppsala. As soon as they entered the place of assembly, the "Happy Hall," they caught sight of the ostentatiously displayed paintings by children of biblical subjects. Their observations were entirely correct. The ecumenical movement today wears a consciously religious dress in contrast to the consciously secular form it maintained between New Delhi (1961) and Uppsala (1968). And the style is continuing to make more and more use of biblical material; it is also using even more dogmatic, liturgical, and typically pious forms of expression that are native to various church traditions from the Greek Orthodox to the evangelical revival movement.

But right in the middle of the midday devotions that I have just described, an atmosphere of self-inflated spirituality engulfed me; it simply oppressed me and made future participation in a third service unthinkable.[51] For, by way of example, I felt that the prayers sung to a saxophone accompaniment were more enchantments than prayers because of their often questionable content; and to call the presence of the Holy Spirit sensibly into a place where people were letting their minds slip struck me as an attempt to manipulate the freedom of that Spirit that blows where He wills (John 3:8). When Gerhard Hoffmann speaks of the *Pentecostal*-pietistic atmosphere of the conference, he reveals a connection which, in light of the number of representatives of older and younger enthusiastic movements actively participating at

---

[51] It is thus a pure fabrication when, for example, Hans Florin contends in his report on Bangkok 1973, p. 3: "He [Beyerhaus] expressed himself to many of us in the last days of the conference as very impressed by the spiritual richness and spiritual course of the conference." In point of fact, I had merely exchanged a short greeting with Florin on the day that he arrived, 8 January, 1973.

Bangkok, is probably very important. It is a connection that deserves careful consideration as a supplementary principle augmenting the experiment in group dynamics. Bangkok struck a note of unhealthy mysticism.

We Protestant Christians in Germany have had our convulsive experiences not only with the political messianism of National Socialism; we also have had, even if to a limited degree, our distressing experiences with the religious fanaticism of the Los Angeles Movement in the events at Kassel and Grossalmerode (1906). It was to these events that the famous "Berlin Declaration" of 1909 addressed itself. We should use the spiritual insights gained through these events to assess with general Christian responsibility these apparently novel characteristics of the modern ecumenical movement. We should consequently make it clear that where another Jesus is proclaimed by another gospel, another spirit is also present there (2 Cor. 11:4). This insight is particularly significant today since through the efforts of Walter Hollenweger attempts are made to reconcile the Pentecostal movement with theological modernism, and, thereby, to bring it together with the charismatic revival and the nativistic prophet movements in Africa — as the enthusiastic type of Christianity into the folds of the WCC.[52]

The Bangkok Conference exhibited strong tendencies to substitute the Holy Spirit by a false spiritualism. Decisive concepts used repeatedly such as "movement, dynamic, process, alteration, sensitizing" point in the same direction. The willful conjunction at the conference between the holy and the frivolous was particularly frightening to me. This was most evident in the cynical witticisms of the conference newspaper, *Yesterday*, in the caricatures and the placard slogans on the bulletin boards, and in the "Celebration of Salvation" on the Evening of Arts that we have yet to discuss. This conjunction had made its appearance as early as Uppsala, 1968, if not officially in the conference program at least in the youth performances on the periphery of the conference. An aspect which frightened me even more in this regard was the observation, not made for the first time, that most Christians today when confronted with blasphemy seem to have lost the capacity to inwardly tremble or to even be able to recognize it as such.

The efforts of an electrical musical instrument, called a synthesizer, served the sensitivity program with technical sophistication. It emitted a clamorous noise at every possible opportunity — the midday meal, the midday devotions, the "Evening of Arts," and the "happenings." These

---

52 Cf. W. Hollenweger, *Enthusiastisches Christentum [Enthused Christianity]* (Wuppertal/Zürich, 1969).

noises varied from the howling of sirens and the clatter of rifles to comical squeaks; they penetrated to the spiritual depths, producing sometimes, terrors, sometimes relaxation or excitement.

On the "Evening of Arts" — during which, as the conference program had it, we were to "celebrate salvation" — four completely unrelated series of slides were projected without explanation in rapid succession on the ceiling of the room with the accompaniment of the synthesizer. In order to look at these we had to sit on the floor. The psychological effect was the complete loss of our capacity for mental concentration. Some felt relaxed and entertained, others got headaches and left the hall. This is in keeping with the observation that, at any given time and according to our propensity for something, our nervous systems react differently to the same stimuli which have been introduced. At the beginning of the celebration an American Negro singer sang a jazz-type hit relating to the salvation theme.

As the high point of this "Salvation Festival" or "Salvation Happening" the entire conference constituency was finally urged by a few Africans to dance enthusiastically with each other. Since the same black participants, as radical adherents of the Black Power Movement or a post-colonial Africa, had only that afternoon indicted us so severely, many European participants felt that the experience was very "liberating and refreshing." This served once again as a kind of absolution engineered by group dynamics. In any case, it was not until the next morning that I discovered the actual intention of this dance when Walter Hollenweger was interviewed on television: the fact that Orthodox bishops, professors of theology, and missionary directors had here danced together, probably for the first time in their lives, has (it was said) changed them inwardly. It has destroyed their prejudices and introduced a process in which they are becoming theologically conscious. The end result will be that missions will also be altered. Here in Bangkok, he said, the new style of future ecumenical conferences has been practiced for the first time.

The conference members themselves had thus been finally and actually wielded together into a single body with homogeneous feelings. And the conference was no longer in the mood to raise essential objections now, given not only the richly filled schedule but also the press for time in which at the end reports were read, briefly discussed, and passed (i.e., sent on with favorable recommendations to the General Assembly which would follow), even if the reports and recommendations contained much that many of them could not actually approve theologically in such form if they had been given time for additional calm examination.

Professor Hollenweger is firmly convinced that the experiment in group dynamics at Bangkok was a first success. In his report, "Professor Unrat Goes to Bangkok," a work written like a novel and shimmering between poetry and fact, he came to the following conclusion: "He [Prof. Unrat] could tally up at least a dozen people who changed radically during the course of the conference."[53]

Hollenweger is perhaps really correct. Perhaps a large number of the delegates were changed, as much in their psychological depths as in their conscious minds, by the experiment in group dynamics at Bangkok. Perhaps they did take home the ecumenical understanding of salvation presented at Bangkok, and perhaps they will champion it there from now on. But this common understanding of salvation at Bangkok did not arise through a process of theological clarification and agreement but through a skilled use of group dynamics. In the language of psychology this is called "engineering of consent," which was achieved with the extensive aid of "subliminal influencing."[54]

Personally I must say that I began to understand truly the course and the pronouncements of the Bangkok Conference only when I started to distinguish two different conferences that were superimposed on each other at Bangkok for a while. Only a few participants and commentators have been able to grasp this. In fact, when I shared this impression with a friend in Bangkok, he was even frightened! But without this view the proceedings of Bangkok did not make sense to me. I knew it like this: The first and crucial conference had begun long before the actual opening of the meeting in Bangkok. It was marked by the constant consultation of the Geneva staff with a firm circle of its trusted sympathizers in other parts of the world. The latter received their personal commitments either as one-time officials of the WCC or as constant participants in world conferences and commission meetings. Many appear to have gotten some skill in group dynamics. Such people are met again and again at strategically important conferences in the various parts of the world and in the most diverse contexts: WCC meetings, conventions of the Lutheran World Federation or the Anglican Consultative Council, the All African Church Conferences, or study meetings of the National Missionary Councils. The first "conference" prepared in advance not only the theology of "Salvation Today" but even the strategy for Bangkok.

The other more representative conference, on the other hand, was the one which the official delegates attended at Bangkok. They were

[53] *Evangelische Kommentare [Protestant Commentary]* (March, 1973), p. 149.
[54] Creegan, *op. cit.*, p. 140.

alertly accompanied and guided at every step by highly disciplined—yet not infallible! — ecumenicals serving as chairmen, secretaries, reflectors, advisors, artists, musicians, editors, or even unacknowledged stimulators in the group meetings. The purpose of this official conference was to arrive as closely as possible, with the aid of the experiment in group dynamics, at the desired results already discernible beforehand in the general report of the CWME and in the addresses of their spokesmen, without at the same time having the delegates lose the illusion that they had prepared these conclusions themselves!

This master plan was partially fulfilled; that it also failed in part was due to defects in organization and also to the still unbroken biblical convictions of a number of delegates from the various countries and confessional traditions. For in spite of everything, and without prejudice to the stubbornly pursued goal of the march, a certain latitude of expression was still allowed. And perhaps the Bible studies which took place in many groups on the three mornings strengthened these delegates in their convictions and immunized them somewhat against the ideological "sensitizing."

It is my belief that this important distinction between the conference of delegates who had some freedom of expression, on the one hand, and the conference planned by the ecumenical organizers, on the other, explains at least in part why the evaluations of Bangkok '73 could vary so greatly, even among those who hold relatively similar theological positions, and even among those who are relatively conservative. In any case this distinction, which I saw as clearly necessary already in Bangkok itself, explains the apparent contradiction that some have tried to prove between my own comments at Bangkok and those made later. My positive observations at Bangkok, and also later, refer to the attitude of the majority of the official delegates who gathered there. It was to these people that I addressed myself in my last public pronouncement at the closing plenary session. I wanted to win them over to my recommendation that we call a conference of responsible missions theologians from the various countries in order to clear up the theological uncertainties in the principles and goals of missions, uncertainties which were manifest even in the documents of the Bangkok Conference. The report of Subsection III B, at the very least, expressed in several places a thoroughly evangelistic consciousness of responsibility for the people not yet reached by the Gospel. But the conference of delegates and their work had no significant authority to influence events in the wider history of the WCC. I had also intimated that at Bangkok itself and indeed precisely in a radio interview which later was used as evidence for my alleged change of mind on my return about the evaluation of the conference:

> My expectation was that a particular view of missions and theology which has been crystallizing for years in the headquarters of the WCC in Geneva, would find broad expression here in the conference through the resolutions that were to be made. I myself, as you know, am not in agreement with this theological direction, and I feared that the results would perhaps even go beyond what we had already experienced in Uppsala in 1968. To that extent, I can say that I am pleasantly surprised about the awareness of biblical priorities which the majority of the delegates have shown during the discussions in the various subsections and which has also found expression in the final reports.
>
> It is, of course, necessary to be very clear-headed here. It is one thing to read what is in the reports and another thing to see what happens to them later. For these reports are not binding in any real sense on the missions office in Geneva, but are at best a kind of stimulus for them. We will certainly have to watch these things very carefully in the future so that the good ideas expressed here do not actually get lost in the shuffle.

In retrospect, I see that I was too optimistic in this interview in my theological evaluation of the section reports. For I had at that time not by any means read them all but had rather constructed my opinion on the basis of my own Subsection III B, which was exceptional, and which basically justified this opinion.

But the decisive matter for me at that time and now is the antithesis, described as early as the interview above, between the awareness of biblical priorities shown by the majority of the delegates and the theological concept of missions as this has been gathering strength for years in the headquarters of the WCC in Geneva. The program actually pursued by the WCC has already been established for years. Its essential elements — openness to non-Christian religions and ideologies, participation in revolutionary movements of our time, breaking off of evangelistic missionary activity by western churches in the Third World — are safely anchored even in the reports and resolutions due to the influence of the ecumenical sympathizers who edited them. This, however, could be recognized fully only later after a careful study of these documents. For frequently the authors of these materials have consciously used ambiguous formulation by which they suggest more than they clearly state, ask questions rather than put demands. Yet the reports do allow a glimpse of the intended positions, and these texts become quite clear when they are seen in the context of the general course of the ecumenical missions movement during recent years. But it is only in the context of all that has been said at other consultations and conferences before and afterward or that is found in countless ecumenical study documents that the reports, recommendations, and resolutions of Bangkok can be correctly understood. Otherwise everything is still ambiguous.

The chairman of the Danish missions council, Bishop Thorkild Graesholt, an official participant at the Bangkok Conference, evaluated the event and the contents of the conference report as follows:

> Bangkok was planned as an experiment in group dynamics. There were only a few plenary sessions. There was too little actual Bible study. There were a lot of meetings which had been predetermined ahead of time. There was an active production of documents whose content had been fixed from the outset. . . . If something or other arose in the deliberations which disturbed the prepared plan, telling oratorical pressure was applied. . . . The people from the WCC were the ones responsible for all the preparations for the conference. It was with their style (I would not like to say flatly a "free style") that we wrote at our meetings. . . . The most remarkable thing about the event was that now and again some parts of the conference refused to align themselves with the grand strategy. But that can be explained by the fact that the gathering was not homogeneous enough for the experiment in group dynamics to be completely successful. It has been said that the meeting was a classic example of a manipulated assembly. I would prefer not to use such strong language. My judgment depends greatly upon how these texts are to be used. But if they are taken as the free expressions of the opinion of the assembly on the various issues, then the game is up. For they were simply the by-products of a not entirely unsuccessful experiment in group dynamics.[55]

---

[55] Th. Graesholt, "Fodnote til en stak dokumenter" ["Footnote to a Pile of Documents"], *Nordisk Missionstidsskrift [Scandinavian Missions Journal]*, 84 (no. 2, 1973), pp. 67, 69, 70.

WHAT WAS BANGKOK'S ANSWER TO THE SALVATION QUESTION?

4

WHAT WAS BANGKOK'S ANSWER TO THE SALVATION QUESTION?

THIS DIFFERENCE BETWEEN the traditional missionary views held by many delegates and the fixed resolves of the ecumenical officials responsible for the conference goes a long way toward explaining the checkered appearance of the section reports. In these can be found affirmations of biblical convictions side by side with penetrating expressions of the contemporary ecumenical ideology. It is quite possible, as a consequence, to construe entirely different pictures of the theological nature of the conference — including even a purely evangelical picture! — from selected citations in the Bangkok reports. And that was how it could happen that even many participants oriented in a basically conservative theological direction returned home from Bangkok with great joy and could report at home that true progress had been made in the theology of mission over the Uppsala Conference. It is our task now to see if such an impression is legitimate.

What then is the *content* of the new understanding of salvation expressed in Bangkok? And what are its most important consequences for the future of Christian missions? The first question is not easily answered in a few sentences. Gerhard Hoffmann in his report in Berlin stated that the Bangkok Conference had propounded no new teaching or slogans in spite of the strenuous efforts of a few western missions people to construct theological statements meant to be comprehensively valid and timeless:

> The ones interested in these things finally succeeded in getting an "Affirmation of Faith" acknowledged in a plenary session. It was a good, pious, and theologically correct testimony which no one could criticize. But in light of the personal struggle which I experienced, particularly in the sub-section which has been mentioned, this "Affir-

mation" appeared to me more like a re-entry visa for certain mission-ary directors who were compelled to bring back something in the accustomed language of Canaan for their constituency.[56]

This is a clear indication from a spokesman appointed by Geneva of how we are to consider those statements in the section reports and also in the Letter to the Churches which sound so biblical and traditionally evangelical. Such statements are useful to the western missionary directors to prove to supporters of their societies that the *status quo* prevailed at Bangkok in all issues having to do with the substance of the faith. As a matter of fact there is a good deal of material in the reports and in the Letter to the Churches to which in its individual segments I could also subscribe. But these are all surrounded by, and even inter-woven with, other expressions advocating much more strongly the con-cepts of salvation which we met in the preliminary study, *Salvation Today and Contemporary Experience* — salvation in the sense of polit-ical liberation, social justice, and women's liberation as well as racial equality and dialogue with people of other religions and ideologies. Some of these things could also be defended by Christians true to the Bible. But inasmuch as they appear here as true salvation, on a par with the salvation offered by reconciliation with God or even replacing this reconciliation, it is disturbing. Other participants at the conference also had this same opinion. For an ecumenical gathering at which a whole multitude of theologians and church leaders of all denominations took part, it is truly a shameful fact that the most penetrating biblical critique of the conference was made by the spokesman of the Roman Catholic delegation:

Not a few participants, the Catholic observers among them, have felt constrained to state that the relationship between the temporal and eternal aspects of salvation was not adequately treated, neither in its eschatological dimension nor in its personal significance here and now. In various ways the impression was left that the effects of the Gospel were more interesting than the Gospel itself. Further, there was too little opportunity to reflect on the foundation of missions, even though the ones who had participated in previous international meetings could have made contributions since these questions had already been exten-sively aired.[57]

[56] Protestant Press Service Documents (6 March 1973), p. 42. The "Affirma-tion" referred to here is printed in the documentary section of this book: 6, B.

[57] *Osservatore Romano [Roman Observer]* (weekly edition in German), no. 9 (2 March, 1973); cited in Protestant Press Service Documents (26 March, 1973), p. 49.

I would like to reproduce a few extracts from the three section reports from Bangkok in the following pages. These will give the reader a personal impression of the theological confusion there. More extensive documentation appears in the appendix. The selections found there expound the main ideas that are particularly typical of the current thought and action of the WCC.

Section I.

Subsection I A, under the direction of Prof. Dr. J. Margull of Hamburg, dealt with the subject, "Dialogue with People of Living Faiths" (i.e., non-Christian religions). Its first main question was: "What is the relationship between salvation in Christ and God's saving work in other living faiths?"[58] Thus stated, the question presupposes without argument that God is savingly active in other religions. The answer in the section report to the question states: "We are conscious of God's movement towards men both as Creator and Savior, bringing man to wholeness and leading him to wider community. . . . Our eyes will be keenly open to discover what he is doing among people of other faiths."

This section, and the conference in general, adopted here the same unbiblical view which the head of the Department for Dialogue of the WCC, Dr. Stanley J. Samartha, had advocated in a preparatory essay for Bangkok:[59] The problem of dialogue amounts to "becoming sensitive to the work of the Holy Spirit in the whole world and that, to be sure, not only within religions but also within the beliefs and ideologies of this world." The ecumenical program of education has here, it seems to me, betrayed its most precipitous aspect: the goal is to make the Christian sensitive (!) for a work of the Spirit in the very place where He, according to Holy Scripture, is never at work (2 Cor. 6:14-17). The serious question arises from this as to what spirit Christians are really opening themselves up to when they enter into this program designed to improve their sensitivity. In any case, for the WCC the goal of dialogue — and this goal is to be increasingly fulfilled through all kinds of missionary activity — can no longer be to bring redemption, but at its best dialogue will function to make adherents of other religions conscious of the work of the Holy Spirit already active in their own religion.

This was the position which Father Murray Rogers advocated unequivocally in the two working papers which he laid before Subsection

[58] Schedule for "Salvation Today" conference (Geneva, 1972), p. 20.

[59] *Evangelische Kommentare [Protestant Commentary]*, no. 10 (1972), p. 593.

I A, namely, "The Spirit: The Milieu of Inter-religious Dialogue" and "Upanishads Study":

> Who then can honestly deny . . . the presence of the fruits of the Spirit even in those who have never heard the Name of Christ or who have never been incorporated into his Mystical Body by baptism? . . . We learn to expect that today also God is speaking to us through the Gentiles' Scriptures, religious traditions, and spiritual experience, indeed, all this is part of his call to us to be more closely and deeply related to him in our life as Christians.

This sentiment is, to be sure, somewhat contradictory to another, rather obscure sentence from the same report, which indicates that there was a division among the members of this subsection:

> Is there an inescapable tension between them [dialogue and evangelism] as some fear? Not necessarily so. . . . A desire to share [on what basis? PB] and a readiness to let others share with us should inspire our witness to Christ rather than a desire to win a theological argument. We were glad to note that increasingly mission is being carried on in this spirit of dialogue without the subsequent decrease in the sense of urgency in evangelism.

The validity of the concluding sentence for the experience of dialogue with the Buddhists is, however, disputed by Manuel Gaxiola:[60]

> One came away from the Conference with the impression that it is the people of the WCC who are most interested in dialogue, while to the others [i.e., the Buddhists] it does not seem a very urgent or needful matter. In any case, we could not detect a positive affirmation of Christian faith in these meetings nor a marked evangelistic desire.

The universality claimed for the saving work of the Spirit is even more clearly expressed in a "meditation" which the report for Section I presents without a special title after its "Litany of Praise and Prayer." The meditation is a compilation of ten modern beatitudes which, with ecumenical generosity, embrace all modern religious, social, and political experiences of salvation — from American Pentecostalism, through Chinese Maoism, to "God-is-dead" theology. The following are among them:[61]

> You were a poor Mexican baptized by the Holy Spirit and the blood of the Lamb.
>
> I rejoice with you, my brother.

[60] Gaxiola, *op. cit.*, p. 70.
[61] Complete text in documentary section: 7, A.

> You were an intellectual Chinese who broke through the barrier be-
> tween yourself and the dung-smelling peasant.
>   I rejoice with you, my sister.
>
> You found all the traditional language meaningless and became an
> "atheist by the grace of God."
>   I rejoice with you, my brother.

Thus for the first time in the history of Christianity an ecumenical
conference has here joined in rejoicing over the fact that someone had
become an atheist, and that even "by the grace of God"!

Dean Walter Tlach said of this: "An atheist by the grace of God" —
and this is not a blasphemous statement? A hundred evangelical passages from the Bangkok texts hardly invalidate this blasphemy."[62]

Section II.

The most important document in which the Bangkok Conference
directly answered the question posed by the conference theme, "Salvation Today," is the preamble to Section II. The Tübingen theologian,
Jürgen Moltmann, was called to Bangkok to compose it. Its third part
speaks of "Salvation in Four Dimensions":

> Within the comprehensive notion of salvation, we see the saving work
> in four social dimensions:
>
> (a) Salvation works in the struggle for economic justice against the
> exploitation of people by people.
>
> (b) Salvation works in the struggle for human dignity against political
> oppression of human beings by their fellow men.
>
> (c) Salvation works in the struggle for solidarity against the alienation
> of person from person.
>
> (d) Salvation works in the struggle of hope against despair in personal
> life.

The conclusion to this part reads:

> We seek the church which initiates actions for liberation and supports
> the work of other liberating groups without calculating self-interest.
> We seek a church which is the catalyst of God's saving work in the
> world, a church which is not merely the refuge of the saved but a
> community serving the world in the love of Christ.

62 W. Tlach, "Kleine Geschichte der Bekenntnisbewegung 'Kein anderes Evangelium'" ["A Short History of the Confessional Movement 'No Other Gospel'"],
idea (24 April, 1973), p. iv.

And the section ends with these words:

> In this sense, it can be said, for example, that salvation is the peace of
> the people in Vietnam, independence in Angola, justice and reconcilia-
> tion in Northern Ireland and release from the captivity of power in the
> North Atlantic community . . .

The politically impartial reader now moves eagerly on to see what, under
these circumstances, salvation means for the intellectually gagged writers in the Soviet Union. But the argument makes a sudden about-face
at the Iron Curtain and directs itself to the inward life:

> . . . or personal conversion in the release of a submerged society into
> hope, or of new life styles amidst corporate self-interest and lovelessness.

Under an apparently biblical and theological dress the concept of
salvation is here deflated and robbed of its Christian particularity in
such a way that every liberating experience can be designated as
"Salvation."

Jürgen Moltmann, the author of the preamble, described this theological concern as follows:

> Prior to the concrete recommendations, Section II on "Salvation and
> Social Justice" developed the only full theological treatment of the
> concept of an *all-embracing salvation* that includes healing of the
> economical, political, cultural, and personal distresses [notice the order!
> PB] of men. It takes up the battle for economical justice, political
> freedom, and cultural renewal as integral movements in the comprehen-
> sive history of God's liberation. It challenges the churches to free
> themselves from complicity with institutionalized injustice, organized
> force, and exploitation in order to become churches that liberate men.[63]

Moltmann's essay bears the title, "Bangkok 1973 — a Mission to Us."
It is in this sense, consequently, that we can understand the idea
articulated in many other reports stemming from Bangkok that Europe,
that is, the European churches, now make up "Mission Field Number
One." The concept is not to be understood in the traditional, popular
sense of missions — as evangelization of the secularized masses — but
as a re-structuring or "renewal" of the churches in a political-economic
sense. Consider in this regard the "prayer" for the "Evangelism Secretary," Dr. Gerhard Hoffmann, the official charged with overseeing
this assignment (p. 79).

---

[63] Jürgen Moltmann, "Bangkok 1973 — eine Mission an uns!" [Bangkok 1973 —
a Mission to Us!"], *Evangelische Theologie* [*Protestant Theology*] (March/April,
1973), p. 212.

By analogy, any participation in a liberation movement can also be designated as "mission." It is this view which M. M. Thomas stated in his introductory address at Bangkok devoted to first principles, "The Meaning of Salvation": "Herein lies the mission of the Church: to participate in the movements of human liberation of our time in such a way as to witness to Jesus Christ as the Source, the Judge and the Redeemer of the human spirituality and its orientation which are at work in these movements and therefore as the Savior of men today."[64]

This thought is expressed in many ways in all the conference documents.

The whole movement lacks clear exposition of the fact that the justification of the sinner is the fundamental event in salvation and that, distinct from this, the readiness to act for better worldly justice is an outworking of the new life. For these later activities may never be placed on the same plane as peace with God. But this has been done in the following sentence from the preamble cited above: "As evil works both in personal life and in exploitative social structures which humiliate mankind, so God's justice manifests itself both in the justification of the sinner and in social and political justice."

The justification of the sinner is even now a finished reality which cannot be surpassed since it involves none of our own work but only God's unmerited act of acquittal. We can never achieve social and political justice completely, and in many situations we cannot even approach it. It will only be a complete reality in the messianic kingdom of peace when the power of the evil one has been removed.

The second critical weakness in Section II's understanding of salvation is revealed here: it offers no explanation of the connection between God's preserving grace in the exigencies of this decaying age and the state of salvation in that world which will come only with the return of Christ, the final defeat of sin and the devil and death, and the new creation.

The "utopian vision" which Pauline Webb, the chairman of this section described, has in fact been translated into an "ideological reality" and a "program of political liberation." These are to be implemented by that church for which the participants in this section and the ecumenical authors of their report were seeking!

[64] M. M. Thomas, "Teilnehmen an der Befreiung" ["Participation in Liberation"], *Lutherische Monatshefte [Lutheran Monthly]* (February, 1973) (no. 2), p. 84.

Section III.

The following statements from the report of Subsection III B on the nature of "salvation" and "mission" were essentially more traditional. Yet even they are still interwoven with ideological and political thinking (which I will accent by italization). This was the group to which I also belonged. A majority of its members, coming from all over the world, saw missions in the essentially classical sense of evangelization and the encouragement of church growth.[65] This cluster of relative conservatives came about as a result of the indulgent arrangements of the Genevan leaders.

Its report contained a series of statements which in their evangelistic concern go considerably beyond the report of Section II at Uppsala. They evidence the fact that their co-authors were evangelicals (Prof. Arthur Glasser and Bishop Chandu Ray). As such, these statements would have been truly welcome if they had not been sucked into a contradicting context which throws their validity into question and finally even threatens to interpolate an alien meaning:

> Salvation is Jesus Christ's liberation of individuals from sin and all its consequences. It is also a *task* which Jesus Christ accomplishes through His church *to free the world from all forms of oppression*. This can only happen if the church is renewed and grows.
>
> (a) Each generation must evangelize its own generation. To work for church growth and renewal is the chief abiding and irreplacable task of Christian mission.
>
> (b) The church may grow in number and in doctrinal understanding, but may lack an awareness of *the call of Christ to participate with Him in liberating society.*
>
> (c) The church may deepen its spiritual life and develop its social services, but may still not hear the call of Christ to pass on His invitation to those who do not know Him, to be reconciled to God. . . .
>
> It is our *mission*
>
> — to call men to God's salvation in Jesus Christ.
>
> — to help them to grow in faith and in their knowledge of Christ in whom God reveals and restores to us *our true humanity, our identity* as men and women created in His image.
>
> — to invite them to let themselves be constantly recreated in this image, in *an eschatological community which is committed to man's struggle for liberation, unity, justice, peace and the fullness of life.*

[65] A. Glasser provides a good description of the meeting and work of this Subsection III B in the "Epilogue" of the volume of essays edited by Ralph Winter, *The Evangelical Response to Bangkok, op. cit.,* pp. 147-153.

The reports from Bangkok are thus so theologically pluralistic that an obviously conservative view of the conference can be constructed through selective quotation, without at the same time having grasped the "spirit of Bangkok." But the witness of the body of Jesus cannot tolerate on equal terms the Word of God and humanistic ideology (2 Cor. 6:14-17). The cancer besetting the spiritual life of our churches today is that a commitment to theological pluralism allows errors that destroy the faith to coexist on equal footing with biblical truths. But this is the very thing that the disciples of Jesus are not allowed to do. When the truth of salvation is called into question, there can be only a passionately zealous Either-Or.

For that reason, it is a fruitless exercise to balance the theological "pros" and "cons" of the different statements in these documents and on the basis of such a discrimination to ground one's opinion of how near the WCC came to biblical truth and the concerns of the historical missions movement at its Bangkok assembly, or on the basis of our analysis how much hope we can still place on further discussions, or what cooperation and clarification are possible between the ecumenical and the evangelical mission movements. For the "Unified Program for Faith and Witness" will not let itself be burdened with any theological and evangelistic statements which do not clearly support their contemporary strategy. In his report on the conference, Gerhard Hoffmann, to whom as evangelism secretary the General Assembly of the CWME had given the responsibility for carrying out the recommendations of Bangkok, expressed himself clearly on the fate of such evangelical efforts as the "Affirmation of Faith"; he called them, you remember, "a re-entry visa for western missionary directors."

The error of evangelical participants at Bangkok lies precisely in this area. In the joy over their success at having interjected a couple of evangelical statements into the final report, they have winked at the much more decisive socio-political reversal in the content of the message of salvation. But in my opinion this very "success" is a serious argument against future cooperation by theologians loyal to Scripture in such pluralistic meetings under ecumenical control. Against their will the participation and cooperation of such evangelicals acts as a stalking horse for the ecumenical propaganda to which it is attached. It is, therefore, much more important to pay attention to the especially emphasized statements which active ecumenical collaborators inserted into the reports by their constant influence during the proceedings, their editorial labors, or even their last-minute insertions than to rejoice over the biblical statements that do appear in the documents.

Against such concentrated and focused action by a cadre — even a small one — a majority of individuals who think otherwise, but who do not interact with each other, is powerless in a plenary meeting since it lacks the capacity to secure recognition and a hearing for themselves. The same general strategy dictated that opinions which dissented theologically were not allowed to be voted on during final discussions of the section reports. At the most, the editorial committees consigned them to supplementary consideration. By taking this course the Geneva leadership retained control right up to the end of the conference, not only over its proceedings but also over its results, and also, consequently, over the first evaluations which have now begun to appear concerning it.

This situation is not at all untypical as a method for ecumenical conferences during recent years. Because of the fragmentation into small study groups, the press for time to discharge reports, and finally the conscious suspension of precision in the wording and character of the proposals, the conference participants no longer really know what business they are doing and what finally will happen to the material under consideration. Added to this is the fact that the greater part of the delegates cannot follow the conference proceedings in their native language and that too much is asked of them by way of parliamentary procedures. As a consequence, all the more authority for planning, final editorial work, as well as evaluation of the conferences, falls to an executive branch that is less and less controllable. It is, moreover, an executive branch which perpetuates itself out of its own midst by an obscure nomination system. The sentence in the preamble of the WCC's constitution, "The WCC is a *fellowship* of churches . . . ," is to be sure still valid in theory. But the actual interdiction of the member churches by the Geneva bureaucracy and its world-wide network of active sympathizers (whom J. Aagaard has called the "third ecumenical movement") presents a disturbing contrast to the theoretical statement.

"Now we are in business," a Geneva staff member remarked when the theologizing conference participants not appointed as delegates to the following General Assembly of the CWME had departed from Bangkok. Now it was time for the structural changes which were necessary in order to implement fully the new concept of missions into the Geneva program. The first concessions of positions were already taking place at the General Assembly of the CWME. Among these was the resolution to change the statement of goals, adopted at New Delhi in

1961, at the next General Assembly of the CWME in 1975.[66] If a delegate from the Philippines had not expressed legal reservations, this would have been done at Bangkok itself. The Geneva executive arm will work for further changes of the evangelism structure in the coming months. The new evangelism secretary of the CWME, Dr. Gerhard Hoffmann, has been specifically commissioned with this assignment. His responsibilities as designated by the General Assembly included also the fellow task, which in light of the conference method strikes a responsive chord: "(4) to give special attention to new ways of communication which imply a sharing of new life rather than of abstract statements on salvation."[67]

In other words, Gerhard Hoffmann, like his predecessor Walter Hollenweger, is to bring the member churches and mission agencies of the CWME into contact with the charismatic movement, to sensitize it through the use of group dynamic techniques, and to continue the process of removing theology from the CWME. To fulfill this task, his colleague, the secretary of the Luthuli foundation, Gabriel Setiloane, offered the following "prayer":[68]

> O Lord, be with our servant Gerhard Hoffmann.
> Give him the patience of an ass
> The health and strength of a mule
> And the perspicacity of a monkey
> So that he may fulfill the mighty task
> of renewing the churches
> and evangelizing the structures for mission!

Thus the real, official, and most influential results of the Bangkok Conference should not be sought in the three section reports of the "theological" conference from 29 December to 8 January, but in the study reports, resolutions, and especially the instructions to Geneva officials at the General Assembly of the CWME which followed from 9 to 12 January, 1973.

At this juncture it is particularly pertinent to point out a recommendation, that is, a resolution, the full text of which is reproduced in the appended documentary section. It is of monumental significance for the ecumenical understanding of "salvation" as this has been expressed at Bangkok and in certain ecumenical circles before and after the conference.

---

[66] Cf. *Bangkok Assembly 1973* (Geneva, 1973), pp. 40, 41.

[67] The complete text of the directing guidelines is found in the documentary section: 8, A.

[68] Bangkok Assembly Document 23, "Report from Committee B, II: 'Guidelines for the Evangelism Secretary'."

I am speaking of the *China Resolution*. It was the product of an evening devoted especially to China, a press conference on China, and also the relevant discussions in the first two sections. In it the General Assembly considers "openness of contact" between Christians of China and Christians of other countries fitting "as and when Christians of China may initiate it." Those who know the situation in Red China doubt that the Chinese Christians who will perhaps receive permission soon for renewed contact with the outside world and with whom the WCC is apparently already in contact are actually representatives of the believing underground church that has been faithful even under heavy persecutions.

In addition, the resolution requested the churches to take the steps summarized in the EPS: "A plea was made for an understanding of Chinese thought in the context of dialogue with people of living faiths and ideologies throughout Asia and for theological and ethical reflection on the transformation of society in China and its implications for other societies."[69]

The background to this recommendation is ultimately the conviction held by many conference participants that God Himself has been at work in the Red Chinese Cultural Revolution. During the China evening one of the speakers compared Mao to the Pesian King Cyrus and called him God's Messiah for the Chinese. The fact that Mao, quite unlike Cyrus, has almost exterminated the people of God in China was of course not mentioned. Addressing this fact at the press conference devoted to China, Philip Potter reassured us that the Chinese Christians of whom he knew had themselves called their experiences in the Revolution "a baptism of fire" and had challenged Christians outside of China to themselves be prepared for such a "cleansing baptism." According to the interpretation of noted ecumenical leaders, the Red Chinese have had a salvation experience which is completely equal, if indeed not superior, to our western understanding of salvation formed under the influence of pietistic or confessional models. It has, consequently, great importance for the future. Philip Potter also stated at that press conference that modern China has something to teach us about the kingdom of God.

Jürgen Moltmann reported in a similar vein about Bangkok:[70]

> The Asians' concern was ultimately the *New China*. Prof. Takanaka who grew up in China compared the extent of the changes in China

[69] Ecumenical Press Service (18 January, 1973), p. 10. The complete text of the China Resolution is in the documentary sections: 8, C.

[70] Moltmann, "Bangkok 1973 . . . ," *op. cit.*, p. 213.

to a miracle. The Orthodox Father George from Kerala, India, wanted to see Maoism in China (not in Europe) as an "invisible church" and asked that the goal of a "classless and casteless society" be included in a conference paper. The theological interpretation of, and practical relationship to, the Chinese Resolution is certainly the most important problem for many Asian Christians. It is *the* challenge for Christians to take up, to the degree that they are free to do so in their countries.

This viewpoint was also expressed at China-study sessions organized in Denmark and Germany. A China consultation was held on 12-15 March, 1973, by the German Protestant and Catholic Missions Councils in Arnoldshain. One participant reported in a personal letter:

> Viewed as a whole, I felt that a few of our brothers, an unfortunately large number of them, were under something like an enchantment which I could not fathom. I cannot identify it any further but it did seem rather frightening to me. There was in all this an all too positive evaluation of Maoism and its relationship to the Christian faith.

And church president Gaxiola had this to say about Bangkok's attitude toward China:

> Although China was very much in the delegates' mind, and a special plenary session was devoted to it, nobody would think of the 800 million Chinese as likely candidates to accept the Gospel nor would they think that God can open a way so that many Christian churches can be established there. In fact, when this possibility was mentioned by the writer to a high official of the CWME, he quickly snapped: "Leave the Chinese alone. They don't need us."[71]

This same attitude found extreme expression in a placard posted by an anonymous hand on the bulletin board of the "Happy Hall," our assembly place in Bangkok. It hung there for several days until I took it down at the end of the conference and brought it along for reporting purposes. This was what it said: "At China meeting — Did you notice the compulsive neurosis of the West to 'convert' China? Salvation — God save China from 'conversion'!"

If this were valid, one could say something like the following which Dr. Arne Sovik mentioned to me while going by this sign: "God save the world from conversion!" That his remark correctly interpreted the opinion of at least a few circles was indicated during an incisive radio report which Hans-Joachim Girock gave on 21 January, 1973, over the Southwest German Radio Church program in Baden-Baden. He first of all saluted the fact that as a result of Bangkok the ascendancy of occi-

[71] Gaxiola, *op. cit.*, p. 75.

dental theology and of western churches and missions had been re-
nounced by the delegates of the Third World. In addition, the course
of the dialogue begun so hopefully with the Buddhists called into question the traditional missionary motive of conversion as well as the
absoluteness of Christianity altogether: "Missions are dead in the classical sense of missionary work among the heathen and conversion. But
for this very reason mission in a new sense has become all the more
important." It now means "even the willingness to relinquish the
claims of Christian absoluteness, to look for, and actually carry on discussions with those of other faiths." In Bangkok only the "tip of the
iceberg" has become visible.[72]

With this point of view the other proposal of the CWME now
becomes even more explosive, and it will perhaps have the most far-
reaching consequences. It is the proposal for a *moratorium*.

[72] Cf. also H. J. Girock, "Konnen diese westlichen Kirchen geheilt werden?
Bangkok — oder die Spitze des Eisbergs. Bericht von der Weltmissionskonferenz"
["Can these Western Churches be Saved? Bangkok — or the Tip of the Iceberg.
A Report from the World Mission Conference"], *Mitteilung für Mitarbeiter der
Evangelischen Landeskirsche in Baden* [*News Letter for Co-Workers of the Pro-
testant State Church in Baden*], no. 2 (1973), pp. 23-26.

WHAT IS THE BACKGROUND OF THE MORATORIUM?

5

WHAT IS THE BACKGROUND OF THE MORATORIUM?

THE ECUMENICAL PRESS SERVICE (EPS) of 17 January 1973, summarized the results of the discussion at Bangkok about a moratorium in its list of "Resolutions of the General Assembly of the Commission for World Mission and Evangelism" as follows:

> A possible moratorium on the transferring of funds from the mission agencies to the so-called receiving churches was seen by the Assembly as a chance for the churches requesting the moratorium to work with their own resources and find their own identity. It would also free the "sending" churches to use their money for new approaches to education for mission among their own people and for those struggling for freedom from unjust and dehumanizing systems.

The communication alludes to the report of Study Committee of the CWME General Assembly which dealt with the concept of "partnership."

Its section B, reproduced in our documentary appendix (pp. 177-179) treats the "Call for a Moratorium." Its actual words were:

> Churches no longer able to send money and personnel will be freed from the traditional, institutionalized missionary enterprise to use these resources for new approaches to education for mission amongst their own people. They will also be freed to give financial support to those struggling for freedom from unjust and dehumanizing systems perpetuated by dominant nations and bodies.

To be sure, the suggestion in this form was not elevated to the status of an official resolution by the General Assembly of the CWME, but it has been reproduced as such by the EPS in its report of 17 January 1973. In point of fact, this "Call for a Moratorium" is energetically supported by well-known persons in the WCC and its ally, the All-African Church Conference. Immediately upon its publication, many men and women thinking responsibly about missions were deeply distressed. The Munich missiologist Prof. Dr. Horst Bürkle, for example, addressed himself to the members of the German Protestant Missionary Council on 26 February 1973, in a circular letter in which he requested them to answer the following questions among others:

(1) Should those who from now on find themselves prepared for missionary service be rejected and the offerings which have been given for their service be returned because of this newly resolved mandate? If not, this requirement must be denounced . . . .

(4) Should we from now on withdraw our personal and financial contributions from our sister churches in order to become the new partners of the groups combatting existing political systems? If not, then we have to send a clear refusal to follow the resolution urging us to exchange our partners.[73]

The answer requested by Prof. Bürkle has not as yet been received; or at least no satisfying answer has appeared. Mere allusion to the fact that the moratorium is a plan involving merely a temporary adjustment of western aid in particular situations in order to develop a mature partnership cannot dispel the unrest felt by the churches that up to now have been "sending" churches.

Anyone who has followed the debate in back of this knows that the discontinuation of missionary sending demanded by the authors of this proposal is meant to be much more radical. The catch-phrase, "moratorium," was introduced in statements by the general secretary of the National Church Council of Kenya, John Gatu, who was later invited to Bangkok. As early as the year before Bangkok at a missions festival (!) of the Reformed Church in America he had given an address on this subject which was widely distributed among the WCC.

John Gatu's address in America began with the trenchant words: "In these remarks I am advocating the positions that the time has come to withdraw foreign missionaries from many parts of the 'Third World,' that one must allow the churches of the 'Third World' to find their true identity, and that the continuation of modern missions constitutes an obstruction to the independence of the church."

John Gatu first proposed that this retreat take place within at least five years. Toward the end of his lecture he sharpened his thoughts even more: "I would like to go even farther and say that the missionaries should be withdrawn, period."

Gatu's reason for this demand included, first, the need of the African

[73] Protestant Press Service Documents (26 March, 1973), pp. 61, 62.

churches to find their own identity as well as the need to rethink the future nature of interchurch relationships. A wealth of partially justified, partially generalized reproaches were raised against the traditionally patronizing attitude of the western missionaries. Gatu demanded the liberation of the Third World "from the slavery of the West" and felt himself constrained to oppose the "imperialistic attitude of the West which holds that it has something which it must share with its fellow-men." To the contrary, the churches of the Third World must develop their own spiritual potential and be themselves occupied with the "mission of God in their own regions." In conclusion, moreover, Gatu goes beyond these reasons to fix a positive goal which gives his ideas an extra dimension. It is necessary "through the withdrawal of missionaries and money from the churches of the Third World for us to prepare for a true transformation, not only a new relationship but also a new conception of the church in which we acknowledge the necessity for change. The Gospel will then have a deeper and more comprehensive effect than our missionary Christianity has had up to now."

To the uninitiated listener these statements sound at first like an articulated hope for a spiritual reformation of the African church with which one could agree wholeheartedly. But someone who knows how to read these sentences in the mirror of contemporary ecumenical efforts toward a new garb for the understanding of the Gospel, the church, and missions can recognize immediately in these sentiments all the charm-words of the new ideology taught at group dynamical indoctrination seminars. The spread of these ideas has been the special task of the Ecumenical Institute of Chicago and the Urban Industrial Mission, which also developed in America. Both of these groups have, it turns out, held concentrated sessions in Nairobi, Kenya. Theirs is the ideology of world change, aided by a fully "renewed church," in which the Gospel has become essentially a socio-political program.

These ideas have not arisen spontaneously in the African churches. They were foreign to John Gatu himself seven years ago when I visited him in Nairobi, December, 1965, in the head office of the Presbyterian Church. At that time I had a long talk with him during which I took notes. We discussed this very question of cooperation by western missionaries with the African churches. He definitely rejected the idea of their gradual withdrawal. That would certainly lead to the destruction of the ecumenicity of the church, he said to me at that time! John Gatu was still able to recall this conversation well when I mentioned it to him in Bangkok, without at the same time being able to explain satisfactorily to me what, in the last analysis, had caused this change in his convictions. This was a change which had also surprised some of his own Presbyterian friends.

In this connection a remark made by the Tanzanian Bishop Kibira at the assembly of the Lutheran World Federation in the middle of May, 1973, in Santiago, Chile, becomes of interest. The idea of the moratorium — which Kibira himself rejected emphatically — was, he said, thoroughly discussed in Cully, Switzerland at a meeting of the WCC Committee on the "Ecumenical Exchange of Personnel" between representatives of the WCC and some Africans in September, 1972, put in writing, and then executed in Bangkok according to plan.[74]

The comment by the general secretary of the South African Christian Council, John Rees, given in an interview in Berlin also agrees with this: "The moratorium is a matter for discussion; it does not really derive from Africans and Asians but from 'missionary societies with troubled consciences' in Europe and North America."[75]

To further illuminate the background of the demand for the moratorium it is profitable to study the notorious "Barbados Declaration — For the Liberation of the Indians." This document was the product of a symposium on Barbados, an island in the Antilles, which was organized in January, 1971, by the ecumenical "Program for Combatting Racism" of the WCC's Commission of the Churches for International Concerns and also by the Ethnology Institute of Bern University. Latin American ethnologists were the most numerous participants. The initiator and major source of financial support for the conference was the World Council of Churches. It did, to be sure, state afterward: "The opinions expressed by the participants are not necessarily [!] those of the organizers." The comment by Prof. Dr. H. W. Gensichen of the German Protestant Missions Council about this reservation rings true: The broad public will see this as simply a protective device to save face for the WCC."[76]

The Barbados Declaration may be taken as quite a typical expression of the attitude of many ethnologists, but, never to that time had a church agency co-sponsored a document so inimical to missions. The document included the following statements:

> The missionary presence has always implied the imposition of criteria and patterns of thought and behavior alien to the colonized Indian societies. A religious pretext has too often justified the economic and human exploitation of the aboriginal population.

[74] Confidential communication from a letter by a German participant.
[75] *Berliner Sonntagsblatt Die Kirche [Berlin Sunday Paper, The Church]*, p. 4.
[76] *Das Wort in der Welt [The Word in the World]*, no. 3 (June, 1971), p. 73.

The inherent ethnocentric aspect of the evangelization process is also a component of the colonialist ideology and is based on the following characteristics:

(1) its essentially discriminatory nature implicit in the hostile relationship to Indian culture conceived as pagan and heretical;

(2) its vicarial aspect, implying the reification of the Indian and his consequent submission in exchange for future supernatural compensations;

(3) its spurious quality given the common situation of missionaries seeking only some form of personal salvation, material or spiritual;

(4) the fact that the missions have become a great land and labor enterprise, in conjunction with the dominant imperial interests.

As a result of this analysis we conclude that the suspension of all missionary activity is the most appropriate policy on behalf of Indian society as well as the moral integrity of the churches involved. Until this objective can be realized the missions must support and contribute to Indian liberation in the following manner. . . ."[77]

In spite of the reservations expressed publicly by the German Protestant Missionary Council, the Department on World Mission and Evangelism of the WCC has still not clearly disassociated itself from this document. The document goes far beyond a concern to criticize — be that criticism justified or unjustified — the historical behavior of missionaries in Latin America. It places the essence of missions fundamentally in question and indicts it as "a component of the colonialist ideology." The call for a moratorium instigated by the CWME at Bangkok in the manner described above can also be understood as an echo from Barbados. For in its motivation, censure of the imperialistic complicity of missions and contention for the Third World churches identity played crucial roles. In any case, it was an echo opposite that which "a broad public" had expected!

Considering all this, it is a deceptive understatement designed to pacify mission-minded congregations to state later that the Bangkok report merely resolved: "That CWME provide study material for discussion of the moratorium proposal as a possible strategy of mission in certain situations as well as information on case studies."[78]

This resolution, apparently so harmless, is in fact nothing less than the "tip of the iceberg" (H. J. Girock) which has peaked above the

[77] *International Review of Mission*, no. 3 (1973), pp. 270, 271.

[78] Response of the six Bangkok participants of the German Protestant Missions Council and the Protestant Study Group for World Missions to the Frankfurt Position Paper of 2 March 1973; in Protestant Press Service Documents (26 March, 1973), p. 32.

surface. Underneath are hidden much more serious activities and developments. The representatives of the All-African Church Conference and of the national church councils of Africa invited to speak at Bangkok saw no further possibility whatsoever for missionary service in Africa. The general secretary of the All-African Church Conference, Burgess Carr, who before holding this position had for years been an official of the WCC's department for Inter-church Aid in Geneva, highlighted the moratorium demand at a Bangkok press conference with these words: "We do not want your money for it is corrupt; we do not want your people for they prevent our leadership from developing; we do not want your power for it makes us corrupt."

Eberhard le Coutre has not without justification pointed to those "on our side of the globe" who calmly put up with such demands "as the rituals of ecumenical conferences that have come to be more or less expected" and yet who "know very well that they will later be sitting at the same tables with their accusers to discuss requests, programs, and projects."[79] In actual fact the rejection of western money and "western power," expressed at Bangkok with such effective rhetoric by those ecumenical officials from Afro-Asian organizations, needs to be taken with a grain of salt since they receive their salaries essentially from western money. The nationalistic rejection of western missionaries is, however, unmistakable. Some of the further reasons for this rejection, as given in the following comment by Burgess Carr, remind us of certain themes which we have already seen in the Barbados Declaration:

> We are in fact not tools, instruments, or raw materials that need to be worked up by other people or through which they gain their own salvation. The history of the missionary movement, especially among the conservative evangelicals, reflects a desire to lead Africans to a salvation that is based in the missionary's own effort to gain his own salvation. All that is now past, all that must be thrown out of the window. . . .[80]

Nothing escapes this condemnation. And the decisive words of the recommendation as originally proposed, a recommendation modified greatly by the resistance of certain section members,[81] of which I was

---

[79] E. le Coutre, "Mit unserer Macht ist nichts getan . . . Versuch einer Anleitung zum Verständnis der Konferenz 'Heil der Welt heute' in Bangkok" ["Nothing has been done in our own strength . . . An Introduction Attempting to Interpret the Conference on 'Salvation Today' in Bangkok"], *der überblick [the survey]* (March 1973), p. 13.

[80] "Afrikanische Kirchenführer zur Presse in Bangkok" ["African Church Leaders Meet the Press in Bangkok"], *der überblick [the survey]* (March 1973), p. 15.

[81] Prof. J. Verkuyl also remarks in his book on Bangkok, *op. cit.*, p. 80: "There was in general little enthusiasm for such a moratorium."

one, read: "We recommand that the Commission seek to provide for the widest possible study and discussion of the call for moratorium as a strategy of mission."[82]

The impression was occasionally left that after all was said and done the western missionary societies should no longer manage their own resources themselves, but should transfer them either directly to the African councils or even to the WCC itself, especially to its program for combatting racism. But what hitherto unknown concentration of power would that lead to?

It is of course questionable whether the older churches are willing to meet these demands. "A lot of conservative churches will withdraw their money if this sort of thing goes through," the Canadian Archbishop Ralph Dean said after his return to Toronto. He was greatly agitated by the extremely nationalistic attitude of Potter and other spokesmen for the Third World in Bangkok.[83] The Finnish missions secretary, Henrik Smedjebacka, in a similar manner, protested vigorously against the connection affirmed at Bangkok between mission societies and the structure of colonial/neo-colonial power: "I believe, to the contrary, that the headquarters of neo-colonialism is in Geneva. . . . The power which the secretaries of the WCC rebuke the old missionary organizations for holding is the very power they would like to have themselves."[84]

More alarming even than the moratorium recommendation itself — for there are certain cases where it is perhaps worth discussing — are the reasons proposed for it in Bangkok and even named in the Ecumenical Press Service: first of all, the Afro-Asian churches are to "find their identity." This means, in the context of the discussion which Section I carried out on "Culture and Identity" and with regards to the so-called "Black Theology,"[85] that these churches should develop a new understanding of Christianity according better with their own religious and cultural backgrounds. The Kimbanguist church of Central Africa was proposed at Bangkok as a notable example. This cult believes that it has received a special revelation and a special blessing of the Holy Spirit through the prophet Simon Kimbangu. In the eyes of his followers he is almost regarded as one of the Trinity. His movement was advanced as a conspicuous example of a truly indigenous African church that has spread rapidly and found its true identity without the cooperation of white missionaries.

82 First draft of the report of Subsection III A, Bangkok Documents, no. 27, p. 3.
83 *Canadian Churchman* (March 1973), p. 2.
84 *Kyrkpressen [Church Press]*, no. 6 (1973), p. 7.
85 Cf. in the documentary section the extract 8, A.

But now, in addition, the money saved by the proposed moratorium and the release of men and women are not perchance to be applied to the support of pioneer missions in areas not as yet evangelized. If this were so, the moratorium idea would be as old as Protestant theory of missions, that is, 120 years old. But missionaries are not. the focus of discussion, and the missionary offerings are now to be set aside for "new ways of mission education." That is, the supporters of missions at home are to be indoctrinated with the ecumenical understanding of salvation and missions, as expressed for example by the support for militant liberation movements, above all in southern Africa.

This is certainly no apparition born of an overexcited imagination or a malicious misreading of the actual facts. We have seen both the indoctrination and the redirection of funds in Germany within the last two years. During 1971-72 we experienced indoctrination for a new understanding of missions in many addresses at mission meetings and during the "Information Campaign for World Mission," organized by the Hamburg Board on Mission.

And even the first phase of the Anti-Racism Program was funded by the reserve funds of the Geneva Department for World Mission and Evangelism, funds which in turn had been accumulated essentially from the contributions of the German Protestant Missionary Council. Antonio Neto, a representative of the People's Movement for the Liberation of Angola (MPLA), an organization operating with Red Chinese training and weapons, was even invited to Bangkok expressly to further this project. In an interview with the magazine, der uberblick (the survey), Neto summoned the German churches particularly to support the "campaign to better inform and modify public opinion" and "in so doing to share their part in human salvation."[86]

In this new view of salvation our overseas sister churches are replaced by communistic trained and equipped guerilla movements. The proclamation of the Gospel is replaced by the revolutionary struggle to overthrow existing structures of authority in Africa and Latin America.

"Out with all the white missionaries!" — This was a slogan displayed in 1971 on placards of the Information Campaign for World Mission. "We should actually rejoice over their departure," the text of the campaign went on to say.

We are now in a position also to understand what the new director of the Commission for World Mission and Evangelism, Emilio Castro, a Latin American representative of the "Theology of Liberation," meant

[86] March 1973, p. 21.

when he summarized the results of Bangkok in the following pithy maxim:

> "We are at the end of a missionary era and at the very beginning of the world mission!"

He himself explained this statement with the following words:

> We have heard here harsh words on the missionary enterprise. But now it is more than emotion — it is theological reflection. The affirmation of African culture, the conveying of Indian spirituality, the challenge to social revolution are the starting points for a new day in world mission. The cry for help from brothers and sisters in Europe, the expression of concern for world mission by delegates of socialist countries invite us to a new day.[87]

In addition to this New Day for missions in the Geneva sense, the Bangkok Conference also heralded the end of the missionary age. No one observed this more sharply than the reporter for *Mission Intercom*, a Roman Catholic magazine in the United States:

> In the debate, the mission confided by Christ to all his disciples was not considered; the world with its expectations and needs was overlooked; the biblical message was not invoked; the intentions, devotion and love of the missionaries, with their mistakes and methods, were not taken note of. . . .[88]

Thus, the Bangkok Conference was meant to achieve nothing less than the replacement of the biblical and historical understanding of salvation and missions by a syncretistic ideology of changing the world, which formed the heart of nearly every recommendation. And by so doing the fundamental crisis of missions was "resolved" by exchanging the very foundation of missions.

That leads us to our next question: How was the fundamental crisis of missions treated in Bangkok?

[87] Ecumenical Press Service (18 January, 1973), p. 2.

[88] Mission Intercom (published by the United States Catholic Mission Council), no. 26 (June-July, 1973), p. 4.

HOW WAS THE FUNDAMENTAL CRISIS
OF MISSIONS HANDLED IN BANGKOK?

6

HOW WAS THE FUNDAMENTAL CRISIS
OF MISSIONS HANDLED IN BANGKOK?

As I TRAVELED TO Bangkok I still held out the faint hope that at least a foundational debate concerning the biblical and theological justification for such an altered understanding of salvation and missions could take place there. Even before the conference it had been requested that all participants present their contributions for discussion with complete openness. It was, accordingly, announced afterward in the "Letter to the Churches": "All of us, freely and in confidence of good fellowship, have been able, and have known how, to voice our own concerns, sufferings and hopes. The dialogue was frank, without compromise and challenging for the future. . . ."

In actual fact, however, the situation did not present itself like that to me. A few of us had recognized, even at the beginning of the conference, that the Geneva organization was unwilling to allow a systematic analysis of the actual theological conflict swirling around the salvation issue or an open confrontation on the question. Prof. Dr. Arthur Glasser (Dean of the School for World Mission at Fuller Theological Seminary) and I — regarded by the Genevans as probably the most radical representatives of conservative-evangelical mulishness — were shunted off into the most conventional of the subsections. This subsection, III B, dealing with "Church Renewal in Mission," also produced the most evangelical sounding final report. But our sights were set higher than that — namely, on a fundamental, theological clarification in the plenary sessions of the whole soteriological theme of the conference. We therefore seized the first and only opportunities for a debate on principles — Glasser on 31 December and myself on 1 January. These were the one and one/half plenary sessions following the three addresses by the ecumenical leaders (Thomas, Potter, and Wieser) devoted to first prinicples.

97

We expressed regret over the fact that the most central issue in the salvation question — namely, the conflict between the ecumenical and the evangelical understanding of missions as this had been described in the Wheaton (1966) and Frankfurt (1970) Declarations — had not even been referred to once in the director's summary covering events from Mexico, 1963, to Bangkok, 1973.

Dr. Glasser was rebuffed immediately by the general secretary of the East Asian Church Conference, U Kyaw Than. As a reliable ecumenical associate from the Third World, he had probably been briefed on how to confront this expected situation much as in soccer a tenacious defender will be assigned to "screen out" the other team's high-scoring center. In any case I learned later in India that Geneva had previously made effective use of U Kyaw Than in similar situations as "a spontaneous voice of the Third World" to counter disagreeable opinions expressed by western theologians. This was his rebuff: "It is well-known that when European theologians sneeze, American theology catches pneumonia. Please keep us from having the Asian churches catch tuberculosis! This is a conference in Asia. Please allow us Asians to set up the conference schedule ourselves!"

When on the next day I addressed myself in the course of a detailed contribution to discussion to this viewpoint,[89] which did not sound very ecumenical to me and which in point of fact reversed cause and effect, I received my rebuke from Philip Potter, the new general secretary of the WCC, himself. Shaking with agitation, he first addressed me privately (I was sitting in the front row right next to him); and then in an *ex cathedra* pronouncement before the whole body he reproached me passionately for trying to work over once again a matter to which he had already directed so much attention. For this, he said, was a purely West German theological dispute. "I would like to call your attention to the fact that the theme of this conference is 'Salvation Today,' not the Frankfurt Declaration!"[90] By purposefully stirring up personal as well as racial resentment, Potter succeeded in mobilizing sufficient emotional support from the Third World participants to be able to put out the fire which had threatened to break out over first principles.

My actual proposal to the conference — to convene as soon as possible an international forum of ecumenical and evangelical theologians in an open and friendly spirit to set about the common task of solving the fundamental crisis in missions — was simply ignored. When I repeated

[89] Documentary section: 5, A.
[90] Documentary section: 5, B.

this proposal on the last day of the conference, and this time consciously without reference to the Frankfurt Declaration, it was not even put to a vote in the plenary assembly even though my last speech to the body had been cheerfully received. It is admittedly true that during the first discussion some Afro-Asian participants opposed the insertion of the Frankfurt Declaration in the Bangkok agenda (something that in fact was never proposed). It is a real question how representative these opinions were in light of the fact that they came from members of the East Asian and All-African Church Conferences, organizations which are bound closely to Geneva by personal, financial, and ideological ties. On the other hand, Dr. Nababan, the acting general secretary of the Council of Indonesian Churches, expressed strong approval for my proposal to hold a later consultation. This was no accident, for my invitation to Bangkok had been arranged by the two general secretaries of the Indonesian Church Council. After I had informed them about the background of the Frankfurt Declaration in July, 1971, they wanted to give me the opportunity to present my views on the fundamental crisis of missions to the conference.[91] But in spite of this real and unqualified invitation, Philip Potter did not give me the opportunity. In fact, the opposite occurred — by his emotional speech, a speech which alarmed many participants,[92] Potter precipitously closed the debate that had only just begun.

At the end of the congress a Korean delegate asked Potter why he had not followed up my request for an international conference since he as well as other leading Asian theologians would warmly welcome such a conference. Potter replied that the WCC no longer considers conferences devoted to doctrine valuable. "We need action-oriented conferences today!"[93]

It has been a conscious act on my part to describe this dramatic episode in such great detail; it was in fact an incident which stirred up strong feelings in the first days of the conference and which then was highlighted in reports of the world press. For by so doing, and by

[91] Cf. my book, *In der Inselwelt Sudostasiens erlebt [Experiences in the Island World of South Asia]* (Stuttgart, 1973), pp. 123, 124.

[92] Cf. Peter Wagner, "Disneyland at Bangkok?," *Evangelical Missions Quarterly,* 9 (no. 3, Spring, 1973), p. 131. Bishop Graesholt, *op. cit.*, speaks of "demagoguery in its purest form."

[93] Personal oral communication from Dr. Chul-Ha Han, Seoul. Cf. also with this statement, W. Müller-Römheld, *Philip Potter* (Stuttgart, 1972), p. 74: "With a certain apprehension Philip Potter saw the strong emphasis of the work on belief and church order in the WCC and the inclination of the affiliated churches to intensify this emphasis under the new general secretary. To Potter the study aspect did not seem decisive, but rather the common action of the churches."

appending the text of my speech as it appeared in the conference newspaper on 2/3 January 1973, I mean to refute the false report which has
been obstinately spread that I demanded the Frankfurt Declaration be
made the focus of the proceedings at Bangkok![94] I was not concerned
with the Frankfurt Declaration but with the ecumenical-evangelical
conflict it discusses, and my recommendation did not deal with the
Bangkok Conference but with a request for a later consultation between
ecumenical and evangelical theologians, a proposal, moreover, with
which the acting chairman, the Indonesian general secretary, Dr. Nababan, was in agreement. It was, however, this very thing which was
flatly refused by the highest officials at Bangkok. And with this refusal
the faint hopes that remained to have a meeting of the minds between
the two opposing viewpoints on the theology of missions and the two
corresponding world missionary movements were destroyed.

The behavior of a few West German delegates was disappointing, if
no longer surprising after the experiences of the debate over missions
in Germany within the Protestant Missions Conference and Council.
When Walter Hollenweger, as editor of the conference newspaper,
Yesterday, asked them to comment on this disagreement, some answered
that they had remained silent in the debate because they were in complete agreement with the speech by U Kyaw Than. "Indeed they feel
that there is no point in bothering an international mission conference
with this document. And in fact, none of the members of the German
delegation have signed it."

Bishop Class, who saw the situation with greater understanding, had
a different opinion. He requested the representatives of the overseas
churches not to delude themselves by thinking "that the problems
addressed in the Frankfurt Declaration are purely West German
concerns."

For the rest, the two German delegations from West and East gave
no perceptible stimulation to the proceedings of the Bangkok Conference. The practice of acting as Reformation-style watchmen that
had been exercised so mightily by such men as Karl Heim, Martin
Schlunk, Walter Freytag, and Karl Hartenstein at the historic World
Missionary Conferences from Jerusalem (1928) to Willingen (1952)
was not continued here at Bangkok, as indeed it had not been at Uppsala
in 1968. As early as our preliminary meeting in Stuttgart shortly before
our departure in December, 1972, it was determined that the West

[94] This was even the contention of J. Verkuyl in his Bangkok book, *op. cit.*,
p. 89: "He demanded — to be sure in the most polite language — that the entire
conference be devoted to the 'Frankfurt Declaration'."

German delegates would travel to Bangkok without theological guidelines from the German Protestant Missionary Conference. The voice of
the church of Martin Luther had grown silent in the ecumenical concert. When Germans do express themselves at WCC conferences,
they usually join in the *cantus firmus oecumenicus* (the common ecumenical refrain).

After returning to Germany the four official delegates of the German
Protestant Missionary Council and the two representatives of the Protestant Board for World Missions once again expressly justified the
way in which Philip Potter and the conference leadership handled
the fundamental crisis in missions at Bangkok. This justification was
contained in a "Reply,"[95] written by the executive secretary of the
German Protestant Missions Council, Pastor P. G. Buttler, as a response
to the "Frankfurt Evaluation" of the Bangkok Conference issued on
2 March 1973.

The signatories of the "Reply" agreed again with the argument of
U Kyaw Than and Potter that the Frankfurt Declaration reflects an
internal quarrel within West German theology which, as such, is meaningless for the Third World. This is a notable contention in two re-
spects. It is first of all an admission of bankruptcy regarding the
meaning of their own, certainly "western," theological labors. If it is
true that "a cough from German theologians could lead to tuberculosis
in Asians," then the preamble of Section II of the Bangkok Report is
also condemned, for as is well known it was drafted by a West German
theologian. It was even conceived in the same building where the
Frankfurt Declaration was drafted! In the second place, the signatories
of the "Reply" knew well, and still know, that the fundamental theological crisis in missions addressed by the Frankfurt Declaration is a
description of the fundamental crisis, or rather the fundamental adul-
teration, in the theology of the WCC. As such it cannot be viewed as
a purely West German problem but one of concern to the whole
world. It would be impossible to single out any of the ideas or challenges of the Frankfurt Declaration as especially "West German"; all
of them have their direct parallels in the contemporary concern by
Japanese believers as well as Americans, Indians, or Dutchmen for
biblical-kerygmatic principles! The fact that the Frankfurt Declaration
produced a spontaneous echo in all the countries of Asia and that
Asian theologians translated it into their languages proves decisively
that its concerns were not parochial.

In addition, one of the most dangerous tendencies of the present

[95] Printed in Protestant Press Service Documents (26 March, 1973), pp. 27-35.

WCC in its disparagement of theological thinking and doctrinal controversy as "western." Theology, when it is genuine, is neither western nor eastern, but biblical; it is the development of the Logos tou theou (the Word of God). Our theology and preaching, as recorded in our confessions and great hymns, are themselves the products of constant reflection by the Church of Jesus Christ in all times on its apostolic and prophetic foundations. This is a process of reflection in which Asia, Africa, and Europe have worked together.

What is then the alternative to "western" theology? In Bangkok, as later at a symposium in Geneva held at the beginning of May, 1973, we were offered a so-called "Black Theology."[96] But this is really nothing more than a conglomeration of ideas drawn from modern — and western! — theologians as well as the ideology of the Black Power Movement. It is a political program written in theological language. In this sense it is really not a theology, and it is therefore not even accepted by the African churches.

Yet it is now the actual desire of leading ecumenical circles to fuse Christianity with "African culture" or "Indian spirituality" as rapidly as possible. The end product is to be nothing less than a giant syncretistic unity that in turn is to pave the way for a coming universal church. For this reason the need to propound exegetically and doctrinally defined theology with clear limits has never been as pressing as now! But the effort to hold an international consultation on these dangers — dangers which many other people beside the authors of the Frankfurt Declaration have described — was once again consciously hindered at Bangkok. And in so doing the ecumenical movement has consistently maintained its accustomed pattern of behavior.

The "Reply" contends that the wish expressed in a resolution by the CWME's General Assembly for strengthened ties between it and "conservative evangelicals" (who do they actually mean by this term?) is a substitute for a discussion of the issues raised by the Frankfurt Declaration. But is this really the case? This desire is certainly not new; it echoes a resolution made at Uppsala in 1968.[97] But the British missiologist, D. Webster, said at that time concerning such a desire: "The right hand of fellowship which Uppsala held out to these evangelicals will not be grasped while its left hand holds the Bible so lightly."

The desire by the WCC for contact with the evangelicals certainly does not arise from any readiness to let the evangelical insistence upon

96 See documentary section, 7, A.
97 Cf. Report from Uppsala, p. 193.

the authority of Scripture, the importance of soteriology, and eschatological preparedness act as the correctives it so urgently needs. It is rather of a piece with a purposeful and partially successful strategy to embrace the evangelicals in their fellowship. The final result is to be that evangelicals will be brought into line theologically and ideologically as the world confessional bodies have been in our time. With that perception the first editorial on the Bangkok meeting in the leading evangelical journal, *Christianity Today*, commented on the CWME's offer to aid in the formation of the World Congress for Evangelism in Lausanne as an idea "almost laughable."[98]

The fundamental presupposition, also cited in the "Reply," for cooperation with the evangelicals is "that the Holy Spirit works in the world by various means"; but this assertion cannot be found in the Bible. Stanley Samartha of India sees this working of the Spirit as the basis for dialogue and cooperation with non-Christian religions and ideologies.[99] Has Samartha really forgotten that the history of Hinduism presents an analogy to this? Hinduism concedes a relative place to every human religion as long as it yields to its pantheistic presuppositions and to the inclusion into the Hindu system. But according to the Bible, the Holy Spirit speaks through the revealed Word of God and cannot contradict Himself. Christian theology is either purely "evangelical," that is, in "conformity with the evangel" or it is in fact not Christian. Pluralistic co-existence by evangelicals within a WCC dominated by different ideologies is thus out of the question, lest they prostitute themselves together with their loyalty to the Gospel itself.

We have come to the final, but critical question: How should missions-minded Christians react to Bangkok?

[98] Donald Hoke, "Salvation Isn't the Same Today," *Christianity Today*, vol. 17 (2 February, 1973), p. 2.
[99] *Evangelische Kommentare [Protestant Commentary]* (October 1972), p. 593.

HOW SHOULD MISSION-MINDED CHRISTIANS
REACT TO BANGKOK?

7

HOW SHOULD MISSION-MINDED CHRISTIANS
REACT TO BANGKOK?

SOME READERS' SPONTANEOUS RESPONSE to this question may be: "We must press the WCC finally to clarify the biblical principles of missions which were distorted so gravely at Bangkok as they had also been at Uppsala in 1968." But I do not think that this is a feasible course any longer.

If in fact Director Emilio Castro really means what he has said, it would be impossible for us to take the consequences of Bangkok too seriously. I am convinced that the WCC has made up its mind to use all the means at its disposal to close the "missionary age" for all of its affiliated churches and mission agencies, as well as for all other institutions which it influences, and to implement its new understanding of "world mission." To do this it will employ primarily conferences and institutes conducted with the methods used at Bangkok, conferences involving experts in the style of the Barbados Conference, scholarships, inter-church aid programs, structural reforms suggested by Geneva, and its own information service.

The goal of the boldest ecumenical thinkers and leaders has grown increasingly clear: to construct a world community embracing all races, classes, religions, and political systems, united as far as possible under a common world government whose business will be the establishment of world peace. It is hoped that a universal church will be able to pave the way successfully for a universal government. Such a universal church would, however, not only be trans-confessional, it would also be unconditionally open to partnership with other religions and ideologies. The former general secretary of the WCC, Eugene Carson Blake, declared in October, 1970, at the "World Conference of Religions for Peace" in Kyoto, Japan, that the church unity for which the WCC strives is only a first step on the way to the ultimate goal of a united mankind.

Revelation 17:11-15 describes what Christians may expect from such "utopias." As early as 1896, Vladimir Solovyev had provided a procative translation of this apocalyptic vision. His *Short Account of the Anti-Christ* described events of the near future in terms of this passage in Revelation.[100] In the advocates of the ecumenical movement we are encountering today a passionate religious-political view of missions whose ardor, fanned to a new high at Bangkok, refuses to let any objections keep it from its goal. If anyone does stand in the way, he is wooed in a friendly manner, simply passed over as unimportant, or, if these methods are not effective, wrathfully attacked. I harbor no illusions about the possibility of achieving a shift in the ominous course of the ecumenical missions movement through theological discussion.

We, therefore, must look elsewhere for guidelines for our missionary strategy and the still urgently needed clarification of the theological basis of missions. A primary presupposition in this effort must be not only concern for the seriousness of the hour but also the certainty of the final triumph of the Gospel of Jesus Christ at His return. This certainty will give us time after time the calmness, even the joy, we require. We need both if we are to act resolutely as missionaries in this decisive hour of world history. For God, the Lord of both the church and the world, is once again opening many hearts and opportunities for the mission of His Son, Jesus Christ, in regions of the world still unreached by the Christian message.

Even Thailand, the host country for the Bangkok Conference, is today the scene of a great revival movement. The president of the Church of Christ in Thailand gave us a glowing report in the conference's opening service:

> The aim of the Church of Christ in Thailand is to double its membership during the four-year period, 1970-1974. . . . At the present time in Thailand there are many young preachers whom God is using in the work of evangelism. Their preaching is a clear witness to Jesus Christ. As they preach, they invite all who have never received Jesus Christ as their Savior to stand up and acknowledge Him publicly. . . . The Holy Spirit is at work in His church.

Michael Mildenberger of Stuttgart commented on this talk in the conference newspaper, *Yesterday*.[101] "The sermon was very bad and the reference to so many saved souls was a direct affront to the ecu-

---

[100] V. Solovyev, *Kurze Erzählung vom Antichrist [A Short Account of the Antichrist]*, translated into German and edited by Ludolf Müller (Munich/Freiburg, 1968).

[101] The Conference Journal, no. 2 (1 January, 1973), p. 4.

menical effort to encourage dialogue." As mission-minded Christians this criticism will mislead us as little as the pressure for a moratorium on the sending of future missionaries. For it is not the World Council of Churches nor any ecumenical leaders in Africa or Asia loyal to the WCC who makes the final decisions about new missionaries. As long as the missionary mandate, "Go into all the world," is still valid, and as long as the Lord Himself by His Spirit still sends out workers into His harvest, such recommendations as made by the WCC are acts of sabotage against the advancement of God's kingdom. Most Afro-Asian church leaders as well as the churches in Africa and Asia are not at all asking for a recall of western missionaries provided the missionaries are prepared to adapt themselves as partners and to truly carry on missionary work. Thus, for example, when the United Presbyterian Church in America recently offered on its own initiative to recall its missionaries from Korea, the Korean Presbyterian Church requested instead that even more missionaries specializing in evangelism be sent out! And in Korea the number of Christians is doubling every ten years!

Henrik Smedjebacka writes concerning the Bangkok recommendation for a moratorium:

> It is only with great difficulty that I can imagine that young churches in Africa, for example, would make such a proposal. They are constantly telling us that they have open doors at present, but that they do not know what the situation will be like in ten years. They consequently need all the assistance they can get their hands on right now.[102]

And the magazine *Lebendige Gemeinde (Living Church)* reports: "Eight mission societies with which we work in the various continents informed us about their needs for 1973: it came to 850 missionaries."[103] On the other side of the coin, it is worth thoughtful consideration that the only church which has up to now tested a moratorium (under that name), the United Church of Christ in Japan (Kyodan) beginning in 1969-70, has seen its church growth come to a complete halt in recent years.[104]

We cannot, in any case, force an organization that has become disobedient to the missionary mandate to revoke its moratorium resolution. Such a revocation might not even be desirable; if in fact an organization has made it clear that it does no longer trust in the full authority and

[102] *Kyrkpressen [Church Press]*, no. 6 (1973), p. 7.
[103] *Lebendige Gemeinde [Living Church]* (May 1973), p. 1.
[104] Cf. P. Beyerhaus, *In Ostasien erlebt [Experiences in East Asia]* (Stuttgart, 1972), pp. 38-40.

content of the biblical Gospel. What good is a humanistically diluted Gospel for the churches and non-Christians of the Third World?

But what we can do is to be all the more diligent, as witnesses of Christ, to see that the good news of Jesus — the Savior from sin, death, devil, and the law — reaches as many people as possible in all six continents within our generation. And we can begin right in our own neighborhoods and among our own people.

This will also mean that our future support will be given only to those missionary agencies which unambiguously confess this unadulterated and uncompromised Gospel. There are still, thank God, many missions and missionaries who are faithful to their trust today. They exist in all countries of the world. At the imminent International Congress for World Evangelism to be held in July, 1974, in Lausanne, Switzerland, a great number of these will gather to find a convincing answer to the question of the world's salvation and to outline the steps to be taken in obedient fulfillment of this goal.

The events of Bangkok provide the opportunity for organizations who have not maintained forthright theological positions to once again speak out clearly on these matters.[105] Those who support missions have the right to know without doubt if their money will henceforth be used for the conversion of the lost or turned aside to "new ways of mission education" or even used to support communist trained and equipped liberation movements. We must further ask the mission agencies to state unequivocally that they will make every effort in the future to send as many missionaries as possible to the two billion people who are yet unreached and that they will not allocate any of the money entrusted to them for political purposes. Any mission which takes a firm stand of this nature does not need to fear that missionary supporters will lose confidence in them in the future.

Beyond that, we need to find ways and means, and indeed we are finding them, to directly help the churches of the Third World which still require assistance in establishing spiritual and intellectual auton-

---

[105] All of the mission agencies affiliated with the German Protestant Missions Conference were represented directly or indirectly at Bangkok by the delegation of the German Protestant Missions Council, so they too have been affected by all the recommendations and resolutions. In response, the Theological Convention (Der Theologische Konvent) and the Frankfurt Missionary Convention (Frankfurter Missionskonvent) requested the German mission agencies through a public notice concerning the World Mission Conference in Bangkok, dated 2 March 1973, to take an unambiguous position in support of or opposition to these resolutions in the near future. This was requested especially for the unfortunate recommendation for a moratorium.

omy. These churches are today the special targets of ecumenical ideology and strategy. They need to be ready to take up the battle themselves against all errors and syncretistic influences and to champion the validity of the Gospel. The evangelical Theological Assistance Program, the Asian Theological Association, and other institutes in the Third World true to the Bible can help realize this goal. Another effort with the same end in view is the establishment of biblically-based centers for missions research and training. Those who are now weighing the question if they too should heed the inner call for missionary service, deserve our full encouragement.

At the same time, all those who are concerned for missions once more should discover the spiritual weapon of *interceding* for the hard-pressed witness to the Gospel in a non-Christian world. They are performing a ministry which cannot be relinquished. For our Lord and Savior, Jesus Christ, for whose return we long, has said: "Before the end the Gospel must be proclaimed to all nations" (Mark 13:10, NEB), and "Happy that servant who is found at his task when his master comes!" (Matt. 24:46, NEB).

"Happy Hall," the assembly place of the World Mission Conference on the grounds of the Red Cross Recovery Center Svanganivas. (Photo by the author)

Leading members of the World Council of Churches under the direction of Professor Margull, Hamburg, conduct a public dialogue with leading Buddhists from Thailand and Ceylon. (Photo by John Taylor, WCC, Geneva)

(From right to left): Dr. Philip Potter in discussion with Rev. W. Wata-keecharoen (president of the Church of Christ in Thailand), U Kyaw Than (general secretary of the East Asian Church Conference), and General Simatupang (general secretary of the Indonesian Church Council). (Photo by John Taylor, WCC, Geneva)

Dr. M. M. Thomas (chairman of the Central Committee of the WCC) presents his address on principles, "The Meaning of Salvation Today." (Photo by John Taylor, WCC, Geneva)

Princess Poon Pismai Diskul (President of the World Fellowship of Buddhists) receives Mrs. Takeda Cho (Asian president of the WCC). (Photo by John Taylor, WCC, Geneva)

Prof. Dr. Jürgen Moltmann, Tübingen, in discussion with Prof. Dr. Walter Hollenweger, Birmingham. (Photo by John Taylor, WCC, Geneva)

New Year's Eve service of the conference participants by candlelight in the open air. (Photo by John Taylor, WCC, Geneva)

Caricatures by the Japanese theological student, Yushi Nomura, who pillories Nixon's cruelty in the Indo-China War and the spectator role of the conference participants in Bangkok. (Photo by the author)

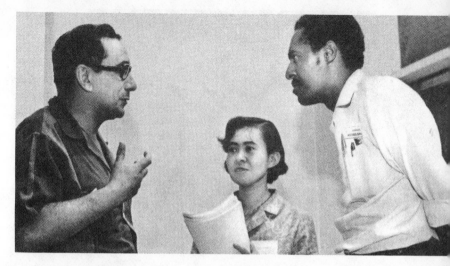

Dr. Emilio Castro (director of the CWME) in discussion with Akiko Yamaguchi, Japan, and the Pentecostal preacher, Herb Daughtry, USA. (Photo by John Taylor, WCC, Geneva)

Conference participants at the "Celebration of Salvation" on the "Evening of Culture." (Photo by John Taylor, WCC, Geneva)

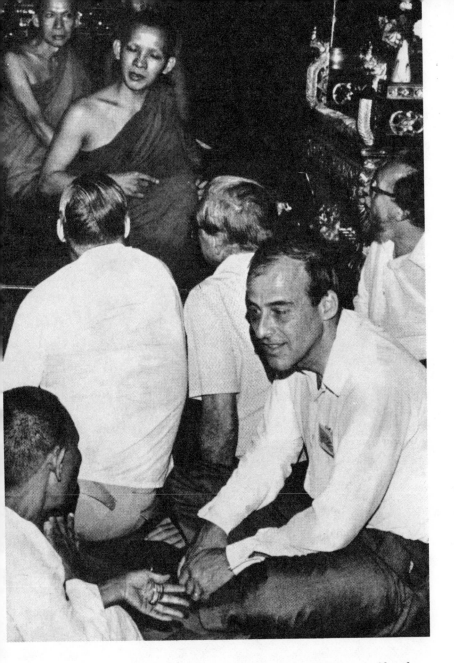

Dr. Lukas Vischer (director of the Commission for Faith and Church Constitution of the WCC) and other conference participants in dialogue in a Buddhist monastery near Bangkok. (Photo by John Taylor, WCC, Geneva)

DOCUMENTS

FROM THE PREPARATORY STUDY MATERIAL
FOR THE BANGKOK CONFERENCE

A. George Johnston, "Should the Church Still Talk About Salvation?"

(From *International Review of Mission*, LXI [January 1972], pp. 241ff. This entire issue of the IRM was devoted to the theme, "Salvation Today," as the October, 1968, issue had also been. In these special issues ecumenical theologians from different continents published their views on the subject. The following is an extract from the most theologically radical essay of this issue, written by the dean of the faculty for religious studies at McGill University in Montreal, Canada. The IRM is the official organ of the Commission for World Mission and Evangelism of the WCC and until recently has been edited by Philip Potter; its editor is now Emilio Castro.)

* * *

In this essay I want to raise the question whether "salvation" is not indeed a biblical word wholly at home inside the Church, but foreign to the society in which we live. Should not the Church abandon it rather than qualify it by ambiguous adjectives like "secular"? . . .

Almost everywhere, however, the word salvation or its equivalents in other languages would conjure up pictures of the Salvation Army at work, of a Billy Graham rally, or of any preacher who is accustomed to plead with sinners to make their peace with God and "accept Christ as personal Lord and Savior."

And yet in large assemblies of people, aye, even in church at Mass or at Sermon in this year of grace, not many are going to devote their entire attention to what the clergy call "sins," be they never so pious. In our part of the world we are worried about the possibility of violent revolution, the present level of unemployment, the recent switch by the USA to protectionist trade policies in what can be described as realistic but cynical self-interest. Some of us are concerned about mixed marriage problems (e.g. of a Jewish man to a nominally Roman Catholic girl), about the reorganization of School Boards and the future of the French language in Canada, or about the fortunes of a favorite sports team (depending on the time of the year and the state of the weather): matters of that sort.

It is not otherwise, I imagine, in Bergen, Norway, or Helsinki, Finland; in Clydebank and the upper reaches of the Clyde at Glasgow; in the Basque country or in Normandy; in Rio or Sydney or Saigon or Amman, whatever the multiplicity of local factors that characterize each situation. Except in a minority of cases within or without the Church, the concerns are health, work and wages, food for tomorrow, finding shelter from disaster, the girl on his mind or the young man in her life, the worry whether the children will go to an early death under imperialist or capitalist or some other tyranny.

That being the case, the Church may well hesitate to stress in liturgy or doctrine the key concept of Paul: "I have complete confidence in the gospel: it is God's power to save all who believe . . . " (Rom. 1:16). This vogue is debased if not outworn; the words do not speak to our condition.

Moreover, talk about salvation is tied to an outmoded religious psychology. A preacher not long ago began his sermon by quoting a Cardinal Archbishop of the Roman Catholic Church, to this effect: the Cardinal was asked what was his chief concern in life, and he replied, "To save my soul." The man in the street can only be puzzled by such language. Of course, it fits in well with the dictionary definition as "the saving of the soul, the deliverance from sin, and admission to eternal bliss wrought for man by the atonement of Christ."

Yet here we have pietistic language from a leading Catholic who operates with the familiar system of traditional Christian truth. . . .

It is with no intention to be discourteous or to "knock" the faith by which another man lives that I have now to say that saving my soul does not interest me as a man in 1972. It is too difficult to talk any longer in terms of the dualism of body-spirit or flesh-spirit. Man is a psychosomatic unity in process of maturing. Unfortunately, this unity is very frail and constantly under threat from inner tensions and from other selves. Deliverance from sin brings up the problematic of God; eternal bliss conveys almost no meaning. Atonement by Jesus on our behalf is just as implausible since He is so distant in history and so unlike most of us. The Church will have to reckon with the probability that the salvation of contemporary man's soul is no urgent issue for him.

Perhaps one should stay awhile with the point just touched on above, that atonement wrought by Christ often has been preached with undue emphasis on the past reference. It was "once upon a time" that Christ died for us. Here is a statement that seems to be historical because it refers to a datable event, yet the "Christ . . . for us" actually sums up a mythological definition of what the event means to a believer. In John 1:29 his meaning is expressed symbolically by the Baptist's words, "Behold, the Lamb of God, who takes away the sin of the world" — an image that is common in cathedral glass, on church banners, in the liturgy, and in great Christian art. But the Lamb of God idea is certainly no more at home in the modern urban world than the claim that Christ wrought atonement for us by dying on a cross. . . .

My point is that salvation, understood in the traditional way, has indeed ceased to be intelligible to many people today.

It was once possible to preach confidently in the language of Paul and Silas (Acts 16:30f.), to invite men to believe in the One who had come and would come again to judge the living and the dead (Acts 10:42). Those who responded could then be washed in baptismal waters in a sacrament that involved (a) turning away from the past, (b) getting a grip on the Savior Christ in the present, and (c) waiting with eager hope and expectation for the eternal bliss that lay ahead in a not too distant future (cf. Rom. 6:1-11; Phil. 3:8-11). They were *saved* — the truth of the myth had come alive. They were still *being saved* — for the new age still overlapped the old and the devil lay in wait to receive them. And they *hoped to be saved*, when Christ returned, when the kingdom of God truly arrived.

Sophisticated theologians of an earlier day, like B. F. Westcott and C. A. Anderson Scott of Cambridge, England, knew how these tenses of salvation could be held together in the thought of Paul and ought to be bound together in any systematic exposition of the Christian doctrine of reconciliation. But it is quite difficult today for the average believer or the modern preacher to maintain this threefold nexus. The Lamb on the window or in the painting is a quaint unfamiliar symbol. The idea of a Second Coming of Jesus as Lord Christ and Royal Judge is wholly unbelievable except as a myth that may not wisely conserve a truth that is worth conserving.

Meantime there seems too frequently to be a harking back to Calvary, season by season dwelling on the wonderful life of the God-man as the Liturgy moves from Advent to Easter, day by day (in some cases) calling out *Kyrie eleison, Kyrie eleison, Kyrie eleison,* if only because the realities of present experience do not bear out the affirmation that in some past — Christ's or our own — we *were saved.* Personal and pastoral practice alike point to the ongoing power of evil that corroborates the rhetoric of Romans 6:1 and 15, "Are we to continue in sin that grace may abound?" "Are we to sin because we are not under the law but under grace?"

Of course I am exaggerating. But the Church cannot afford to ignore the difficulty that in 1972 the distant "once upon a time Christ died for my sins" strikes even a veteran theologian of the Atonement like Emeritus Professor James S. Thomson of McGill University, as something that is hard nowadays to justify. . . .

B. Shusako Endo, "The Priest and the Apostate."

(This is the last selection in the anthology, *Salvation Today and Contemporary Experience,* which was published by the Commission for World Mission and Evangelism of the WCC as the most important preparatory document for the Bangkok Conference. It is an excerpt from a contemporary Japanese novel which takes us back to the time in the 17th century when Christians were persecuted in Japan. A young Portuguese priest wants to find his teacher, Ferreira, who due to torture from the Japanese authorities has abandoned his faith. In this effort he himself is imprisoned, and Ferreira from outside the prison now speaks to him. This excerpt is from the book by Shusako Endo, *Silence* [Tokyo, 1970], pp. 267-271, English translation by William Johnston.)

"Now they are in that courtyard." (It was the sorrowful voice of Ferreira that whispered to him.) "Three unfortunate Christians are hanging. They have been hanging there since you came here. . . ."

"When I spent that night here five people were suspended in the pit. Five voices were carried to my ears on the wind. The official said: 'If you apostatize, those people will immediately be taken out of the pit, their bonds will be loosed, and we will put medicine on their wounds.' I answered: 'Why do these people not apostatize?' And the official laughed as he answered me: 'They have already apostatized many times. But as long as you don't apostatize these peasants cannot be saved."

"And you . . ." the priest spoke through his tears, "you should have prayed. . . ."

"I did pray. I kept on praying. But prayer did nothing to alleviate their suffering. Behind their ears a small incision has been made; the blood drips slowly through this incision and through the nose and mouth. I know it well, because I have experienced that same suffering in my own body. Prayer does nothing to alleviate suffering. . . ."

To chase away the imagination he kept banging his head against the wall. "In return for these earthly sufferings, those people will receive a reward of eternal joy," he said.

"Don't deceive yourself!" said Ferreira. "Don't disguise your own weakness with those beautiful words."

"My weakness?" The priest shook his head; yet he had no self-confidence. "What do you mean? It's because I believe in the salvation of these people. . . ."

"You make yourself more important than them. You are preoccupied with your own salvation. If you say that you will apostatize, those people will be taken out of the pit. They will be saved from suffering. And you refuse to do so. It's because you dread to betray the Church. You dread to be the dregs of the Church, like me." Until now Ferreira's words had burst out as a single breath of anger, but now his voice gradually weakened as he said: "Yet I was the same as you. On that cold, black night I, too, was as you are now. And yet is your way an acting love? A priest ought to live in imitation of Christ. If Christ were here. . . ."

"For a moment Ferreira remained silent; then he suddenly broke out into a strong voice: "Certainly Christ would have apostatized for them. . . ."

"No, no!" said the priest, covering his face with his hands and wrenching his voice through his fingers. "No, no!"

"For love Christ would have apostatized. Even if it meant giving up everything He had."

"Stop tormenting me! Go away, away!" shouted the priest wildly. But now the bolt was shot and the door opened — and the white light of the morning flooded into the room.

"You are now going to perform the most painful act of love that has ever been performed," said Ferreira, taking the priest gently by the shoulder. . . .

"Sawano, is it over? Shall we get out the *fumie?*" As he spoke the interpreter put on the ground the box he was carrying and, opening it, he took out a large wooden plaque.

"Now you are going to perform the most painful act of love that has ever been performed." Ferreira repeated his former words gently. "Your brethren in the Church will judge you as they have judged me. But there is something more important than the Church, more important than missionary work: what you are now about to do."

The *fumie* is now at his feet.

A simple copper medal is fixed on to a gray plank of dirty wood on which the grains run like little waves. Before him is the ugly face of Christ, crowned with thorns and the thin, outstretched arms. . . .

"Ah," says Ferreira. "Courage!" . . .

The priest raises his foot. In it he feels a dull, heavy pain. This is no mere formality. He will now trample on what he has considered the most beautiful thing in his life, on what he has believed most pure, on what is filled with the ideals and the dreams of man. How his foot aches! And then the Christ in bronze speaks to the priest: "Trample! Trample! I more than anyone know of the pain in your foot. Trample! It was to be trampled on by men that I was born into this world. It was to share men's pain that I carried my cross."

The priest placed his foot on the *fumie.* Dawn broke. And far in the distance the cock crew.

C. **"The Salvation of the World Today," a Round-table Discussion in Geneva.**

(Transcribed from the tape of a discussion involving approximately fifteen leading ecumenical mission theologians from all over the world.)

MC: Yesterday we lived in a safe world. That is what the Beatles sing. What about our salvation today? This is the question which made men and women, scholars and missionaries, church bureaucrats and bishops from the whole world and from all confessions consider. First, they compare the sound and the concept of the word *Salvation* and *to save* in several main cultures. Second, they try to understand the theological meaning of the pluralism of salvation against different cultural backgrounds. Third, they discuss the possibilities of open-ended and closed theological systems and ecclesiologies. Fourth, they try to come to certain conclusions. First, Dr. Nabahan shows the connection between the Indonesian word *quslamatan* (salvation) and the Hebrew word *Shalom* (peace):

Dr. Nabadan: In the Indonesian language, the word for salvation is *quslamatan* and it has same root with the greeting word *salamat* from the Arabic root. The meaning of this word is first of all *peace*, politically and socially. Peace includes also joy, enough food, no trouble and a free life — free especially from fear and from ghosts.

MC: The Indian word for salvation is connected with the Sanscrit word *moksha*, coming from the root *mook* and then *muchatae*, to release, to free.

Dr. Samartha: It would mean, therefore, that in seeking *moksha*, man is trying to break out of the bondage of karma-sansara, that is a cycle of births and deaths to which he is attached. *Moksha* also means freedom that comes after release from this bondage.

MC: Beautiful songs of salvation have been created in recent years in Swahili, expressing *salvation* in African tradition. (Music) Mr. Nicholas Maru from Tansania comments:

Maru: The swahili word which is equivalent to "save" is *acore*. It just means *rescue, deliver*. It's as simple as that.

MC: The Finnish word for *salvation* is *balasta*, which means "saved" from something such as a storm. But the noun used for *savior* is not *balastaya*, but *bactayasta*, the one who liberates. Miss Inga-Brita-Castrén from Finland comments:

Castrén: The trouble is that this word *Bactavasta* (the one who frees and liberates to something) has become a purely religious term which is scarcely used in any other connotation or any other connection at all, except in the religious language.

MC: Why do you say all this is "a trouble"?

Castrén: Because the word doesn't say much to modern man; it's a nice, sentimental word without much meaning. It's not used in political language or social discussions at all.

MC: Professor Hans Margull from Germany states that the phrase, "Jesus Saves," is almost unknown in Germany, at least in Luther's translation of the Bible.

Margull: Luther's translation always speaks of making free, of liberating or of bringing salvation and then salvation is something in which a man is incorporated.

MC: Yet the word *heil* has a rather dubious history in Germany, as it has been stolen and poisoned by the Nazis, although its original meaning, which is connected with *hellin*, which means "healing," and *heilis*, "holy," is a very broad and open-ended concept.

MC: In the Slavonic language of the Russian Orthodox Church, the word *salvation* means deliverance from an inevitable destruction. (Music)

Potter: When in our theology we speak of salvation, we understand an enormous effort made by man. And according to the effort he makes, our Lord gives him strength. These two sides, the free will of man and God's help, are the conditions for achieving salvation.

MC: Dr. Tracey Jones from the United States understands salvation in the same way as the Finnish speaker; that is, "taken out of the storm and placed safely on the beach." (Man sings: "Blessed assurance, Jesus is mine. Oh what a foretaste of glory divine.")

Jones: If the understanding of salvation is limited to this, I would find it not sufficient for my own understanding of what has happened to me.

Another voice: "And how do we keep our balance? That I can tell you in one word — *tradition*." (Singing, which ridicules tradition.) Dr. Jones continues:

Jones: But if you take the root word of salvation as I understand it, there is also within it not only deliverance and liberation from evil (these are very important today), but also, the whole idea of healing. The saved man is the man who is being made whole. He is the person in a·world of tremendous mental anguish and internal storm of all kinds. He is the one who is being healed within himself and therefore can also help in a healing process with others.

MC: The Rev. Philip Potter, comparing these different understandings with the Old Testament concept of salvation, leads us into the second part: namely, the theological meaning of the variety of these concepts. (Music).

Potter: The Hebrew word for salvation is *yeshua* and it comes from a word *Yasha*, which in Semitic languages means a lot of what has been said around the table so far. It means *to make wide* or *spacious*, to release someone who is confined or imprisoned, in any way, whether through illness or whether through want — someone who is hungry and is released by being fed — or someone who is held back by enemies and is released (delivered) or who is being oppressed by others and is released (delivered) through the manifestation of justice. Therefore, the rulers, the kings and all those who have power have it as their duty to be saviors — to remove all those things that hinder people from being free and spacious in their existence.

MC: We have seen that the story of salvation is told differently in different cultures in different parts of the world. Professor Colin Williams tries to find the typology of these different concepts of salvation. In a traditional society, he says (the society in which we have a strong feeling of evil powers pressing in upon people), where it is almost impossible to remove economic and political powers people might find a necessary haven of humanity, a protection from the impersonal powers, in a congregation of Christians.

Williams: When you live in a society, for example, where there might be a great change, as say, with the black people in America at the moment, where there is an awareness that how there is no excuse for just living as liberated people internally, believing nothing can be done about furthering God's purposes, liberating purposes, in the world—in these circumstances the message of Christ the Savior is a call to go out into the world aggressively and change the structures of society so that men, black and white, are freed, so that we are liberated from racism and from injustice, so that the broad life which God intends for all mankind can start to be realized.

The difficulty is that often these different cultural situations seem to be in conflict with each other, so that you have, for example, in certain western cultures at the moment, some Christians who are saying "to be saved is an internal thing; it doesn't mean that you've got to get involved in political and social freedom." But others recognize that the biblical meaning of salvation is much broader and they say "No, if you believe that Christ is the Savior, now the *real* task to be done in our society is to seize the opportunity which God is giving us of breaking through to a more liberating and a more just society."

At first sight these two meanings of salvation seem to be in contradiction to each other, but in the light of the language we have seen around the table here, we can see that the meanings which are offered to us by Christ in different cultural situations can be quite different, but all comes under the one concept of freedom or liberation or wholeness.

MC: This Franciscan subculture is found in unexpected places. Sometimes in new secular forms, like for instance, in Latin America where young people begin to see the Che Guevera and Jesus Christ as belonging to the same tradition.

(Music)

MC: Dr. Sapsezian, from Brazil, sees three reasons for this surprising blend of traditions and Dr. David Stowe from the United States (former head of the Division of Overseas Missionary of the NCC) makes an even more daring comparison between Mao Tse Tung and the example of Christ.

Dr. Sapsezian speaks:

First, for these young Christians in Latin America, the deeper meaning of Christian commitment is, to say it briefly, freedom to give oneself, literally to renounce one's life. This is to be Christian today in the fight against oppression. And a second thing which I find very important for our discussion, is that those young Christians feel that living Christ today is not necessarily dependent upon an explicit personal, relatable experience with Christ. Even if this area is not well defined (like in the life of Che Guevara, who was not a committed Christian) they are nevertheless able to believe Christ. And this is important for these young people. Those who fight for this freedom know also that they themselves will not enjoy the good things now. They are rather called to renounce and to postpone probably, and to die, so that others may enjoy.

Stowe: "I think it is important to note that along exactly the same line as the thinking of the monks and Che Guevara, is the experience of an enormous number of people in China under the influence of the thought of Mao Tse Tung, because surely in the cultural revolution you have raised to an extraordinarily vivid and active pitch precisely this ideology of total self-giving for the sake of the community, the abdication of individual self-interest, and a tremendous confidence that through this kind of self-giving the total historical process will be moved onto a new level of liberation and abundance for everybody, entirely beyond the bound of formal Christianity, but I think reflecting profoundly the operation of this spirit in history."

2. A MESSAGE FROM HER ROYAL HIGHNESS, PRINCESS POON PISMAI DISKUL, PRESIDENT OF THE WORLD FELLOWSHIP OF BUDDHISTS.

(Given at the opening of the World Missions Conference in Bangkok on 30 December 1972. From the conference newspaper, *Yesterday,* of 1 January 1973.)

Mr. Chairman,
Ladies and Gentlemen,

It is really a rare privilege that I am given the opportunity to speak to the congregation of the honorable representatives of the World Council of Churches who have come from various parts of the world to discuss and exchange ideas on the theme "Salvation Today."

First of all, I would like to say that the selected theme is so appropriate for the occasion, being terse, thought-provoking and relevant to the circumstances we now find ourselves in.

The problems and troubles threatening us all at present are many; they need practicable principles and practical persons to tackle them efficiently so that we can be spared their disastrous results. This is *salvation*, for the sake of which our initiative must be taken *today*, from now on.

Although I am a Buddhist professing a different religion from you, yet I can speak from the innermost of my heart that all religions have one thing in common: the ultimate aim of raising a human being above the condition of being always driven by instincts and impulses. In other words, this is to raise him beyond other creatures that walk the same earth and breathe the same atmosphere, making him a being that is "human" in the best sense of the term. All genuine religious people, despite the difference of outward trappings, know that they are heading toward the same destination, the difference being that each has chosen the path he prefers. In this respect the Buddha once said, "Virtuous men understand each other."

And why not? Just study the Tripitaka and the Bible and we shall see the same essence underlining the different wordings of each message: do not kill, do not steal, goodwill toward all and malice toward none, and many others. No founder of any religion that is worth the name, whether the Buddha or Jesus Christ, has ever taught the disciples to hate or to harm other people. Their lives were also paragons of the virtues they preached. What they did always matched what they talked. If some of their disciples had erred or are erring, the fault lies with themselves, not with the religious teachings or religious founders.

Frankly speaking, there is one thing which appears to be universal to all religions today. This is that we tend to attach too much importance to the part of religion that is rites and ritual and at the same time to pay little attention to the teachings that will lead to understanding and growth. This results in modern youth tending to assume that religion is something alien and irrelevant to them. This is a point which I humbly offer to the congregation for the sake of, as you know, "Salvation Today."

Our task is now how to make youth and most other people reverse their trend of thought and admit the fact that religion or, to be more precise, religious practice is indispensable for their own welfare and security, of both the body and the mind. It is through religious practice alone, they must be made to understand, that they can earn them the name of human being in the real sense of the term. Without religion in their thoughts, words and deeds they cease to be human but have only a "being" no better than animals. To this end, it is also necessary that we religious people be living examples and models of the doctrines we preach. Without this foundation the time, money and efforts involved are wasted.

The spirit of living a religion one preaches and of worshiping one's religious founder with practices is, I am glad to say, common to both Buddhism and Christianity. In Romans 12, life in God's service is emphasized. It reads, "Offer yourselves as a living sacrifice to God, dedicated to His service and pleasing to Him. This is the true worship that you should offer."

In Buddhism the Buddha also gave a warning to his disciples before his passing away, saying, "Anybody who practices the Dhamma is worshiping me with the highest kind of worship."

Besides, belief and unbelief, like love and hate, respect and contempt, cannot be forced. Each depends on growth and tendency. It is because of this fact that there are several remedies for the diseased minds. This is to match the growth and tendency of an individual and also the kind of disease he is suffering from. But all spiritual remedies, be they called Buddhism, Christianity and others, produce the same effect for those who take them: recovery from disease and the consequent health, vigor and a greater life. Whether this be called Nirvana or union with God or an eternal life does not matter.

In conclusion, may I invoke the grace of whatever is sacred and divine in the universe: . . . the triple Gem, the Holy Trinity or others, to give us their blessings for our success in the task we are undertaking for other peoples. We live on one planet. Together we orbit in space, breathe the same atmosphere and share the same fate. Our success is therefore their success, . . . and happiness and peace and security, and, most important of all, *Salvation.*

Thank you.

(Delivered in Absentia by the Hon. General Secretary of the World Fellowship of Buddhists, Aiem Sangkhavasi.)

3. AFRICAN DEVOTIONS OF 6 JANUARY 1973, in BANGKOK

Order of Service	*With Notes*
Call to Worship: Songs by Belafonte and Makeba	These are protest songs out of the Southern African situation. The words are *Tula Mama Tula* — quiet mother, quiet — meant to comfort a weeping, brokenhearted mother whose son has been jailed for "being man." *Be Hleli Bonke Etologwene:* There they are (the leaders of the nation) all locked up in prison. Oh, what shall we Africans do! Is there any hope for us?
Announcement of Theme for the worship service	*Unity in Diversity:* In Africa God is experienced by various names among different peoples: Lesa, Mungu, Unkulunkulu, Tixo, Zambe, Mudzimu, yet it is acknowledged that He is the One God. Now it can even be said "The Father of our Lord Jesus Christ," Ruler of the Universe, Destiny of Mankind.
Intercessions	Therefore all mankind comes to Him saying "Out of the depth I cry unto Thee, O Lord."
Hymn	Let us praise the Lord in song: "O Lord, our God."
Silence	Let us listen to the Lord "The Lord is in His temple that all the Earth keep silent!"
Scripture	Ephesians 2:1-10

Meditation (In French)	Jeremiah 31:15-17, by Mme. R. Andriamanjato. The idea is to remind the world that the majority of church membership in Africa is people of the feminine sex. Also the leadership of the local churches is mainly in the hands of women.
Hymn	"Love Divine, All Loves Excelling" (sung to a Xhosa tune).
Silence	Let us again keep silent before God. (The music in the background comes from the Eglise Evangelique Protestant du Cameroun. They tell how "The enemies of God are sad because Christ has won a victory." And "How we are free").
Agape Prayer	Grace for the midday meal.
The Brotherly Greeting	We all sing this chorus from Kenya meaning "Peace, peace be with you all." Shake hands each with his neighbor.
Dismissal	In silence we proceed to the Dining Hall. The silence is broken only when in "the breaking of the bread," we say the word of peace and share God's gift of bread with others.

4. EXCERPTS FROM THE THREE PRINCIPAL ADDRESSES AT THE CONFERENCE

1. Dr. Thomas Wieser, Geneva, "Report on the Salvation Study."

(From I.R.M., Vol. LXII, No. 246, April, 1973, pp. 170-179.)

Selection of the Theme

It may be useful to recall a few of the factors which led to the choice of our theme by way of a general review. There was a certain risk in the choice of the theme, which was made in 1968. Those for whom salvation was an indigenous part of their religious vocabulary might not see any great need to discuss it. Others who were concerned with interpreting the Gospel in the secular world or in relation to other religions might not find it useful to focus on a term which could have an initially alienating effect on those whom they wished to bring nearer to the Gospel or with whom they wished to carry on discussion. One of the first sections at the CWME meeting in Mexico City in 1963 asked: "What is the form and content of the salvation which Christ offers to men and women in the secular world?" But whether the best way of dealing with the question would be to discuss explicitly the term "salvation" was another matter.

As it turned out, the positive reaction to the theme has been considerable and is still growing. . . . The choice of the theme was welcomed as a return to the essentials of the Christian faith and mission, or it was understood as the challenge to make explicit, in the midst of missionary involvement in the world, the basis of the faith. It was furthermore found that in dialogue with people of different religious faiths the notion of salvation, far from being a stumbling block, came into the center of the conversation as one of the points around which the dialogue could be clarified.

This is not to say that there were no critical questions raised. Some conservative evangelicals asked whether the discussion of salvation in the "non-committal" context of an ecumenical discussion would not further dilute rather than strengthen the commitment of Christians to effective mission. In other circles there was concern whether the secularization debate had been prematurely concluded.

1. The Bible, Tradition, and "Salvation Today"

The study of the Bible has been one of the important dimensions in the attempt to clarify the understanding of Salvation Today. Since the theme proposed the "discussion of a particular biblical expression of the Faith as a way of restating the nature and purpose of the mission of God" (IRM, October, 1968, p. 395), it was natural that a great deal of attention should be given to biblical studies.

(a) *The Bible as norm*

However, the question is not only how much attention was paid to the Bible or how much use was made of it, but how it was used. In particular, how was the Bible to be understood as norm and authority for the contemporary affirmation of salvation in Christ? This question was approached in a number of different ways.

The report from a Dutch group speaks of a *cantus firmus*, a continuing theme running through the various writings of the Old and New Testament. The description of the theme follows the main stages of "Salvation History," from the Exodus of Israel from Egypt to the coming of Jesus. The unity of the theme and the continuity of this history provide the power and the authoritative basis on which to proclaim and believe in salvation. But the emphasis on history and historical continuity raises the further question about our place *today* in relation to this history. Does the sequence of saving and liberating events, described in the *cantus firmus*, continue up to the present day?

A straightforward affirmative answer to this question would imply that the coming of Jesus, especially His death and resurrection, represents only one stage in the whole sequence of events. Over against such a relativizing tendency a report from Germany (Oekumenisches Seminar, Tübingen) insists on a qualitative difference between the biblical story and the rest of history, because the "revelation of His plan of salvation can be found only in the particular history of His people Israel and the founding of the Church of Jesus Christ" (p. 5). While the organic unity of the Bible is acknowledged, it also must be maintained that the Old Testament must be read in the light of the revelation of the New.

The insistence on the uniqueness of the story in the Bible in the interest of affirming its authority, however, serves to accentuate the discontinuity between the biblical story and our historical situation today. Does this mean that the authority can be affirmed only when it is one step removed from our experience? . . .

2. Salvation in/and History

(a) *The notion of liberation*

One of the points where the connection between the biblical story and contemporary experience seems to be apparent to many people is the notion of liberating. It would therefore seem a good testing point for the way in which the Bible is used.

Evidence of the increasing use of the word "liberation" in interpreting the meaning of salvation for today is the fact that it also occurs in the reports at the point where salvation in the individual/personal sense is discussed. Thus, the report from Australia mentions "liberation from inward and outward forces of drugs, rampant selfishness, the destructive power of competiveness"; salvation, according to a report from a Polish group, is "liberation from the state of sin, weakness and narrowness of the spirit, all limitations that separate people from God and His grace." The personal and social aspect may also be combined, as in a statement that salvation "means the liberation of man and nature in all dimensions . . . from the material, psychological, political, economic, religious, ideological chains" (Report from the Japanese consultation).

(b) *The need for distinctions*

Others would use the term "liberation" in a more pronounced way as referring to a socio-historical process. To speak of salvation in terms of "liberation" in this sense means therefore to interpret the historical situations and historical processes in such a way as to make it relevant for the process of salvation. We hear warning cries against the use of the term liberation in this sense: does this interpretation of history not blur the distinction, variously defined, between the personal/individual and the communal realm, between the "spiritual" and the political, between the historical/immanent and the eschatological/transcendent, between salvation and humanization?

The effort to arrive at the proper distinction in this respect took up a great part of the discussion in the Scandinavian countries. During a recent consultation it was maintained with reference to the purpose of dialogue that the dialogue between Christians and non-Christians should be confined only to the "humane issues" and was not applicable on the level of, for example, talking about salvation. The presupposition behind this affirmation is a rigid distinction between salvation and humanization. . . .

(c) From creation to redemption

. . . As we attempt to understand salvation in terms of such a comprehensive process we are, of course, not automatically eliminating the distinctions mentioned previously. But we should at least be freed from the pietistic concept of salvation as primarily a private affair between an individual and God. In this connection a German report calls for taking salvation out of the private sphere. Salvation Today cannot mean merely an "individual application of a past event." Today we must seek to "relate eschatological faith to the concrete historical realities in a way that the societal involvement of human existence becomes evident". . . .

3. Salvation and the Church

During the early stages of the preparation for the meeting a major portion of the discussion was supposed to be devoted to the "predicament of the saving community." In the course of the study during the last four years there was considerable discussion about the predicament of the church, but little reference was made to the term "saving community."

(a) The predicament of the church

The reports show various ways in which the predicament of the church is seen. In the German Democratic Republic congregations "face a twofold temptation: since the day-to-day life of the socialist society ignores them, they are tempted either to settle for a ghetto existence, or to allow their actions to be determined solely by the situation, instead of letting the Gospel redirect their action within the situation" (Report of the Working Group). In the report from Australia the problem is described in terms of a credibility gap. "Many people find it hard to believe in the individuals who call themselves Christian . . . . still less do they accept the institutions which use the name Christian. The church's task is therefore twofold: to render itself credible in its visible form, and to fashion a language in which to preach the Christ who is incarnate." Similarly, a report from Japan concludes that "the church, in its course up to the present, has failed to concern itself with the sufferings of this world; with its eyes turned in only upon itself, and without realizing it, it has made the work of salvation into a selfish purpose."

In a Canadian study group the first reaction to the theme "Salvation Today" was: "Is the church not arrogant in thinking it can offer man salvation?" From there it moved on to the search for authentic styles of mission. It concluded that "the institutional church must expose its own idolatrous imagery and superstition if its witness is to be effective." This would involve, in the North American context for example, a much clearer distinction between Christianity and Americanism, or between the Protestant work ethic and the Christian Gospel.

(b) The church and God's saving purpose

In attempting to overcome the predicament in which the church finds itself it is important that it arrive at a true understanding of its role in the saving purpose of God for the world. A report from the Ivory Coast, after stating that the church is the means by which God accomplishes His work of redemption, asks: "Does this mean that salvation is limited to the four walls of the church? Is God not free to act where He pleases? Was there not also a Samaritan among the ten lepers healed by Jesus? . . . Where did Jesus find the greatest faith, if not with the centurion? Did He not say that several will come from the East and the West and will sit down with Abraham, Isaac and Jacob in the kingdom of God, and that the sons of the kingdom will be thrown out? Therefore we would say that all those are saved who, inside or outside the church, believe in Jesus." The insight that God's saving work transcends the walls of the church, because it is the completion of His work in creation, leads to the task of relating positively to the world. "The church has a responsibility to identify and support all secular movements which contribute to the completion and perfection of creation and to the full development of mankind according to the image of God" (Aide-memoire of the Orthodox Consultation). . . .

2. M. M. Thomas, "The Meaning of Salvation Today — A Personal Statement."

(From the *International Review of Mission*, April, 1973, pp. 158-169.)

True and false sacredness

. . . Behind today's revolutionary search for a society harnessing nature for human welfare through science and technology, eliminating poverty and oppression, opening to hitherto submerged groups the door of participation in power structures, and moving toward a fraternity of free and equal persons, is a spiritual creativity which has its source, in part at least, in Christ's salvation of the human spirit. One could speak of it as a new stage in God's process of Creation.

Law, sin and death

But every new stage in Creation has its Fall; and every creativity which turns to false realms of meaning and sacredness becomes self-destructive and betrays the human liberation which it seeks and which is promised by Christ. . . .

It is precisely at this point that the victory of the Cross is relevant. The

mission of the church in this context is to be present within the creative
liberation movements of our time which the Gospel of Christ itself has
helped to take shape, and so to participate in them as to be able to communicate the genuine gospel of liberation — from the vicious circle of sin
and alienation, law and self-righteousness, frustration and death into the
new realm of Christ's New Humanity where there is forgiveness and reconciliation, grace and justification, renewal and eternal life. It is this message
that will liberate the liberation movements from the false spiritual structures of meaning based on idolatrous worship of schemes of self-redemption,
and thus redeem their creative impulses from self-destructive tendencies,
enabling them to achieve their inner rationale of human emancipation.
Our message of Christ's salvation is ever the same; it is the call to men and
nations to turn "from idols to serve a living God" who has "translated us
from the domain of darkness into the Kingdom of his dear Son" Jesus
Christ. In Him we have a divine forgiveness and are delivered from the
ultimate spiritual insecurities of the self that seeks justification through its
own efforts, and are "made free to love." Today "idols" and "darkness"
have a new character; and "love" too must have new implications. . . .

Christianity and other religions

I have spoken of choice between God as revealed in Jesus Christ and
man-made idols in the realm of structures of ultimate meaning and sacredness. This does not and should not be understood to mean a choice between Christianity and other religions. In fact God and idols cut across
this distinction. The criterion is openness and response to the meaning of
life and sense of the transcendent as revealed in the Person of Jesus Christ.
Nor does it mean the choice between religion and atheism. Religion may
be idolatrous, and atheism may be no more than a denial of idols and the
affirmation of an undefined transcendence, which is open to the reality of
the transcendent humanity of the Cross, like the unknown God of the
Athenians and like the modern atheism of Jawaharlal Nehru or some Marx-
ian humanists of Europe at present. This is the Christian rationale for a
dialogue on salvation with people of other religious faiths and secular
ideologies.
  Indeed, we are living at a time when we are deeply conscious of pluralism
in the world — pluralism of human situations and needs, of varied religions
and secular cultures, with different traditions of metaphysics, ideologies and
world-views, in terms of which Christians themselves seek to express their
commitment to and confession of Christ. So much so that any kind of a
unity in the doctrine of Christ or of salvation in Christ, which has been
the goal of traditional Christian churches, is to my mind impossible even
of conception except in religious imperialistic terms. As a historian of
religion, Wilfred Cantwell Smith (*Questions of Religious Truth* [New
York, 1967], pp. 34, 35) has recently said that on the grounds also of the
loss of authority of the established churches today, "the old ideal of a uni-

fied or systematic Christian truth has gone. For this the ecumenical movement is too late," leaving a situation of "open variety, of optional alternatives," everyone choosing what suits him best.

Then, of course, the question is sharply raised of the kind of criterion of
Christian faith which can be laid down in a pluralistic age. Dr. Hans Kung,
when he visited India recently, said that the criterion of faith could be that
the believer should in some form acknowledge the Person of Jesus as
"decisive for life," that is to say, to translate in my terms, decisive for the
knowledge of Ultimate Reality and the realization of the ultimate meaning
of life and its fulfillment here and hereafter.

The place of the church

If the above is true, and salvation in Christ is conceded outside the
church, what is the significance of the church? I have assumed the role
of the church as the essential agent of mission. But what is the church?
What are the essential marks of the self-identity of the church? How
should it be structured to participate in the various religious and secular
communities and in the creative processes and liberation movements so that
it may promote its mission of salvation? This needs to be more fully
explored. But let me just list a few fragmentary and rather unconnected
ideas.

(a) I am personally convinced that the gathering for the study of the
Word and the celebration of the Eucharist is the center of the church's
fellowship. But it is a moot question whether the fellowship should be a
separate religious community among others, where most of the primary
levels of social living of the believers are confined to the Christian circle,
where there is even a Christian law governing their conduct and recognized
by the State, as is the case today in many countries of Asia, and certainly
in India.

(b) In a situation like India where Christian conversion has come to
mean a transfer of allegiance from one culture and juridical community to
another, rather than from idols to God through Christ, and where baptism
has become almost like the old circumcision, how can baptism regain its
true meaning of spiritual conversion? Is it by considering baptism a condition of membership of the church or a privilege of membership?

(c) Recently Wilfred Cantwell Smith has raised the question whether
the word "Christian" should be considered an adjective or a noun. Were
the believers at Antioch first called "Christian" to denote a new quality of
faith or "Christians" to denote a separate communal identity? The answer
to the question of substance involved in it has great implications for the
nature, the methods and goals of our mission. My friend, the late E. V.
Mathew, often raised the question whether it were not better, for the sake
of the Christian mission, that the church form new sects in the sense of
groups with a prophetic and evangelistic vocation, within the movements

of cultural creativity and social liberation, rather than try to bring about one organized Church of India, which may only mean several small ghettos joining forces to form one large ghetto. Here the question is whether we have really grasped the nature of unity in a missionary church.

These are some suggestive lines of theological exploration regarding the nature and structure of the church in the light of its mission and salvation. I leave all these unanswered questions for this conference of experts to tackle.

3. **Excerpts from the Director's Report, Dr. Philip A. Potter, Geneva: "Christ's Mission and Ours in Today's World."**

(From Bangkok Assembly 1973. Minutes and Report of the Assembly of the Commission on World Mission and Evangelism of the WCC, 31 December 1972 and 9-12 January 1973, pp. 51-63.)

The context of mission

We are now living, at an accelerated pace, in one world in which all peoples are drawn together through science and technology, rapid means of communication, and the mass media. Indeed, the great new fact of our time is the coming into world history of millions of hitherto submerged peoples who belong to those areas which have hitherto been called mission lands — Asia, the Pacific Islands, Africa, Latin America and the Caribbean. The news of the world can be heard in every land and can be seen on the television screen while it is happening. People desire and possess the same material things, though this varies widely between the rich and poor within and between nations. Some call this a secular form of ecumenism, i.e. a coming together willy nilly of the whole inhabited earth in time and space.

The fact of one world has held out great prospects for the world mission of the church. The eschatological words of Christ have become very vivid and urgent: "This Gospel of the Kingdom will be preached throughout the whole world (*oikumene*), as a testimony to the nations" (Matt. 24:14). This has created a lively debate in missionary circles as to whether the emphasis should be on proclaiming the Gospel to the two billion or more who have never heard it in the lands which have lived for millenia by other faiths, or whether it should be preached literally to the whole world, including the so-called Christian lands of Europe, North America and Australasia. This debate is totally futile when we look closer at this one world in which we are living.

Our one world is in reality a world which is profoundly divided politically, economically and racially. This is the context in which Christ's words quoted above are uttered. For it is foreseen that "there will be wars and rumours of wars . . . nation shall rise against nation, and kingdom against kingdom; and there shall be famines . . . and earthquakes, in divers places"

(Matt. 24:6, 7). We have witnessed the growing power of the super-states of the USA and the USSR and the development by them of the ultimate means of the destruction of the human race. They have used their power to divide the world into spheres of influence and have been involved in all the tragic conflicts of these years. While the USSR operates on the universalism of a secular, anti-religious ideology, the USA and its allies claim to exercise their power and influence in terms of a democratic ideology which has roots in the Christian Gospel. It is, however, important to remember that the USA deploys more than 60 per cent of the Christian missionary force around the world, and the resources which go with it, while Western Europe and Australasia account for the remaining 40 per cent or so of missionary and Christian service involvement. . . .

Now the Christian mission has from the first been concerned with justice and the welfare of people. The early church in the Mediterranean and the monks in Europe laid the foundations of a more widely based economic and social life, through their proclamation of the Gospel of man's liberation from the forces of nature and from the fear of each other. This tradition has been wonderfully carried forward in the past two hundred years or so by the modern missionary movement from Europe and North America to the rest of the world, through the preaching and teaching of the Gospel, through education, medical care, agricultural and social work. And yet, the facts of the past decade show the continuing appalling exploitation by the rich nations of the poorer nations, even in the name of development. Development has been seen purely in economic terms and that means on the basis of the structures, values and dynamics of societies which adhere to the doctrine of the survival of the fittest. A closer look at the situation shows clearly that the rich nations are spiritually and morally underdeveloped, functioning on the philosophy of aggressive individual and corporate egoism. Development, like mission, must be seen to involve all six continents.

Racism. One particularly virulent form of the political and economic conflicts of our time is racism and particularly white racism. The Mexico meeting took place a few months after the March on Washington to demand civil rights for blacks and other racial minorities. This event and the emergence of liberation movements in South Africa hardly claimed the attention of that meeting, in spite of its direct relationship to mission and evangelism. For it is a notorious fact that the period of the Western mission to the continents of colored people was that of European and North American political and economic imperialism. There were features of the missionary movement which contributed to or reinforced the disease of racism and particularly white racism.

Three years after the International Missionary Council was inaugurated, its secretary, J. H. Oldham, wrote a book, *Christianity and the Race Problem*, in which he analyzed the situation as it then existed and the challenge it posed for the Christian mission. He expressed the challenge as follows:

Christianity is not primarily a philosophy but a crusade. As Christ was sent by the Father, so He sends His disciples to set up in the world the kingdom of God. His coming was a declaration of war — a war to the death against the powers of darkness. He was manifested to destroy the works of the devil. Hence when Christians find in the world a state of things that is not in accord with the truth which they have learned from Christ, their concern is not that it should be explained but that it should be ended. In that temper we must approach everything in the relations between races that cannot be reconciled with the Christian ideal.

Oldham was not present at the Jerusalem Conference on World Mission in 1928 when "The Race Problem" was discussed. But he must have been disappointed by the mild and meager statements which were then made, compared to his call to a crusade against racism in the name of the Gospel of the kingdom of God and His justice. It is significant that at no other world missionary conference was this matter central until the enlarged meeting of the Committee of the Division on World Mission and Evangelism in December, 1969. But as President Kaunda remarked in a meeting in October, 1970, at which were present several Muslim African leaders, the active humanitarian support by the WCC to liberation movements struggling for racial justice had restored for Africans the credibility of the Gospel. Nevertheless, that generous statement by President Kaunda does not take us off the hook regarding the relation of mission and evangelism and the existence of white racism practiced so often in the name of Christian civilization.

Violence. One of the new features we have witnessed in this period of political, economic and racial conflict, has been the awareness of the violence of existing constitutional systems and the counter-violence of those who seek liberation from the injustice of these systems. Christians have been ambivalent about violence, especially missionaries, who, because of being thousands of miles away from home and enjoying the protection of the older colonial power or the new forms of post-colonial rule, found it relatively easy to counsel Christians to non-violent and evolutionary methods of achieving change. The curious thing is that, particularly in the Second World War against Fascism, many missionaries either left their posts to fight against Germany or Japan, or encouraged Christians to pray for the victory of the cause of righteousness — their cause. Today Africans, Asians and Latin Americans see in the repressive attitudes and actions of foreign powers and/or the regimes which rule them, the same elements of fascist oppression. But they are tacitly urged by Westerners to be docile and forbearing. . . .

In recent years we have witnessed a violent reaction to this growing powerlessness of man. The youth and student revolts of the 1960s were a prophetic attack against such irresponsibility and idolatry. It is significant that the churches and their theologians were left either helpless or hostile in face of this reaction, and that for the very evident reason that so much of Christian theology and so many ecclesiastical institutions partake of this irresponsibility and of enslavement to "what is." The heart of the Christian mission was therefore compromised — the fact that through the incarnation, death and resurrection of Jesus Christ, God has made us responsible for His purpose in the world to work for radical change, conversion, salvation, in face of the principalities and powers of nature and of men, so that man may be released to become God's *poem*, "created in Christ Jesus for good works which God prepared beforehand, that we should walk in them" (Eph. 1:15 - 2:10).

Mission in context

. . . There is the further sobering fact that everywhere the churches and their missionary activities are caught in the structures of their societies. The failure to cope adventurously and effectively with the eruptions which have taken place in these years under review has demonstrated very clearly the captivity of the churches and the missionary agencies to the political, economic, racial and cultural institutions of society. The church which would be the bearer of salvation today needs itself to be saved, liberated from all that is false to the revolutionary, convincing and renewing nature of the Gospel. Despite the controversy which it provoked, the section on "Renewal in Mission" at the Uppsala Assembly was right in delineating the church as a priority situation for mission today. . . .

What methodologies are called for in such a situation? The report which lies before you hints at a few methods, and the structure of this meeting itself is a test of these methods. I would like to refer to four of them:

(1) *Dialogue* has become a major element in witnessing to our faith. Perhaps the most significant development in the work of the CWME has been in furthering "the Dialogue with people of living faiths and ideologies." As a program it is regarded as so important as to become a separate sub-unit within Unit I on Faith and Witness. . . .

(2) Mission and evangelism cannot be carried out by supplying a cut and dried confessional and theological bundle of Christian truths. Through the process of dialogue, through give and take, we are in a better position to understand and communicate our faith. An indispensable method is that of *action and reflection* with the participation of the whole people of God. The CWME's studies on the Missionary Activity of the Congregation, Churches in Mission, and more recently, on the Role of Christians in Changing Institutions, the programs of Urban Industrial Mission, the reform of theological education, plans for community health care, and the church's mandate to heal — all these point to more effective means of carrying out our mission and — what is still more important — more relevant ways of communicating the Gospel.

(3) Mission and evangelism are not primarily activities of organizational officials but the concern of the whole people of God. The studies which were developed on forms of pastoral service, theological education, and the missionary structure of the congregation, the strategies which were decisive for the program of Urban Industrial Mission and Mission for Rural Areas (i.e., participation by the people themselves in discovering their needs and those of their society and organizations), the program of Education for Mission, the methods adopted in Helping the Churches in Evangelism, the Role of the Laity Abroad — all these are exercises in facilitating the *participation of every Christian in mission and evangelism*, which ought to be normal practice for all churches and mission agencies.

(4) Partnership has for a long time been recognized as the appropriate way to carry on mission and evangelism. This was stressed previously in Whitby, 1947, and again in Willingen, 1952. But the reality in which this was carried out in the past was different. The partner who has money, knowledge, and education — and this is most often the western partner — still has the power. The partner without these things, who is the receiver, often finds himself in a position of dependence which he hesitates to give up for fear of losing the aid which is so necessary. CWME has in the past ten years emphasized *Joint Action for Mission*; this means that churches and mission agencies in a given place survey their common tasks as well as their resources in personnel and funds for meeting these tasks, and find ways of committing themselves to work together or on behalf of each other. The CWME has carried this concern further by promoting with the Commission on Inter-Church Aid, Refugee and World Service, a new program on the Ecumenical Sharing of Personnel, which asks some very searching questions about the selfhood of churches and the meaning of real sharing. . . .

These methodologies raise urgent issues concerning the structures for the churches' mission today. They must be seen as responses to the context in which we are compelled to witness in the 1970s. But they are also expressions of the Christian message of salvation. Our reflections on salvation in Christ have led us to discern that it is concerned with the liberation of persons and societies from all that prevents them from living an authentic existence in justice and a shared community, and with openness to others and to God's future. Salvation is hope in action — the action of suffering love for and with others that they may share in this free life in Christ. When we compare the context in which our mission takes place and our actual practice of mission and evangelism, we may be tempted to despair. But God's saving act in Christ liberates us from our fears, and enables us to be free to experiment, to be mobile and contextual in our approaches, to sustain each other in love and prayer, and to leave the issue in His hands. In this spirit we will, I hope, make the most of our exacting task in the coming days.

5. FROM THE PLENARY DEBATE IN "OPEN SESSION" ON 1 JANUARY 1973, IN BANGKOK

(*Yesterday*, the Conference Journal, No. 4, 3 January 1973.)

A. The Statement by Prof. Dr. Peter Beyerhaus

Mr. Chairman,

I want to make a few comments on the report of the General Secretary yesterday. First of all I would like to express my gratitude for many important issues which he discussed and from which I have learned a great deal. In spite of this I must confess that I also was disappointed by the report, for Dr. Potter did not touch on one most crucial issue, the development of a theology of mission between the meetings in Mexico 1963 and Bangkok. This period was marked by the infection of the World Missionary Movement by that fundamental crisis of the Christian faith which was pointed out in the opening sermon of the Uppsala Assembly by the late D. T. Niles. It resulted in a growing polarization into two world missionary movements, which often are referred to as the "ecumenical" and the "evangelical" ones. The high points of this development were:

1. The Wheaton Congress 1966 and its Declaration. 2. The great debate in Section II of the Uppsala Assembly 1968. 3. The subsequent publication of the Frankfurt Declaration in March 1970. 4. The organization of world-wide and regional Congresses on Evangelism as genuine alternatives to the ecumenical mission program and conferences.

Yesterday Dr. Arthur Glasser mentioned the Frankfurt Declaration and was met by remarks of the Rev. Kyaw Than, the General Secretary of the EACC, remarks which were not very ecumenical. I find that we should never try to suppress an articulation of faith or also of spiritual anxiety, even if it comes from the West. We are really living in a world of six continents today where all churches should share their joy and sorrow. Mr. Kyaw Than made however an important observation when he spoke of a spiritual infection which has started in Germany and which threatens to affect the whole world. But he confused the cause and the effect, or the disease and the diagnosis. There is indeed today a serious infection of the faith. It is a fundamental crisis: 1. in biblical authority, 2. in the concept of God, 3. in our image of Jesus Christ, 4. in our understanding of Salvation, 5. of the Church, 6. of Revelation, and 7. of Eschatology (compare the seven theses and antitheses of the Frankfurt Declaration).

You can describe this crisis both by the categories of lack and deficiency, i.e., that integral biblical elements of these teachings have been destroyed, or by the categories of infection and falsification, i.e., that the genuine biblical concepts of these terms have been substituted by ideological ones, which are incompatible with the genuine biblical concepts. If this crisis is not tackled very soon it will lead to the total corruption and death of the

Christian Church and Mission. This crisis, it is true, did not originate in the Department of World Mission and Evangelism, but it has seriously affected much of its thinking, speaking and acting. That this is the case could even be proved by a careful analysis of the speeches and Bible studies to which we have listened at this Conference.

The Frankfurt Declaration has called this crisis and its elements by their names. For some people this did not sound very pleasant. Some patients do not like to be told the name of their real illness.

Still, this crisis is not a purely German matter. This was demonstrated by the strong resound from the whole world. Last year I made a journey through the Far East. I was invited by several theological seminaries and church councils to address them, and the first issue demanded by them — not by myself! — was usually an introduction to the background of the Frankfurt Declaration, which already had been translated into Japanese, Chinese, Indonesian and other Asian languages. I could really discover that the crisis of faith has affected churches in the Third World and more specially so their theological seminaries.

It had been our hope — I am now speaking on behalf of the leading theologians amongst the Conservative Evangelicals and of those who issued the Frankfurt Declaration — that the CWME would really take up this burning issue. We had sent the Declaration to the headquarters of WCC and LWF in Geneva, and we had offered to come with a delegation which at an international consultation could interpret the concerns of the Frankfurt Declaration and deliberate about them. We repeated our offer several times. For we held that if the CWME continued to refuse to do so it would resemble a headmaster of a school who is informed about a fire that has broken out on the roof of his school building, but who simply ignores that information and instructs his teachers to go on teaching his children as if nothing had happened.

To our distress between Uppsala and Bangkok nothing has been done to take up such responsible top-level deliberations between the WCC and the international evangelical movement in order to tackle these highly important issues.

The announcement of the Bangkok theme "Salvation Today" raised the hope in us that this would be an excellent opportunity to discuss these central biblical concerns on a highly representative level. But the structure of this conference, its division into many small cells which are not expected to produce statements or reports, has again made it impossible to come to terms on this issue.

Let me therefore conclude by proposing to this Conference that in the near future a top-level consultation be held where both ecumenical leaders and leaders from the non-conciliar, evangelical movement from the whole world in an open and friendly spirit deeply and responsibly go into these burning questions and thereby try to resolve the fundamental crisis of Christian mission. Thank you Mr. Chairman.

B. The Response by General Secretary Dr. Philip A. Potter

(Translated from the German Protestant Press Service E.P.D. Documents, 4/73 of 15 February 1973, pp. 32ff.)

Mister Chairman.

The first remark that I would like to make is to remind this seating that it is on the theme, "Salvation Today," and not on the Frankfurt Declaration. Of course in this Conference we are all open to receive from each other, from different positions, what we believe. That is what we are here for. And the love [which is discussed here] is not a love which has to be used as a word all the time. It is a love which is a total attitude, an atmosphere, and also the willingness to speak to each other the truth in love. Too much of the missionary movement, certainly in my own lifetime, has been spent in saying nice public words or trying to cover up the issues, and I hope that the scene is set here to know that when we speak about love we are speaking about judgment and suffering. And when we speak about love, it is a love which must express itself in justice and true community. And those of us who have had to struggle with the preparation of this meeting and have traveled far and wide around the world know what are those cries of men that this love be manifest in new attitudes of humble receiving and giving of each other. If you look again at all I said about the methodologies that we have sought to employ, you will see that they imply an attitude of love. That's the first remark I want to make.

The second one is to say that regarding Prof. Beyerhaus and his interventions, I did pass some remarks to him personally a while ago, and I have to confess to you that the way he passed them on to you is typical of the way in which our correspondence and discussions have gone on in the past. He has interpreted to you what I said to him in his own way, and that disturbs me. As regards the Frankfurt Declaration, he has told us that it was sent to the World Council of Churches and the Lutheran World Federation and sent for, or been received by a delegation as a world document, and so on. There were a number of bureaucratic problems involved in the correspondence, but the position that we took was this: this document was produced by a particular group of German theologians — of West German theologians. That is the first point. And they were purporting to make this *the* world discussion, and we would not accept that. We were prepared to discuss with them in Germany the issues that were involved there. Prof. Beyerhaus, I noticed, has not said a word about the debate that has been going on in Germany about the Frankfurt Declaration.

The next point I want to make about it is this. Those of you who have read that Declaration will have noticed that it was written in the form of theses, it was written in the form of what we — the writers — affirm and what they deny. And what was intriguing was the way in which they described what they denied. There was no previous effort at a consultation or discussion. It was an indictment that was made, and therefore since the whole thing was conceived, written, and distributed — as you have heard here this afternoon — as an indictment, we chose to treat it in the place where the indictment was made. I was interviewed about it, and it was published.

Prof. Beyerhaus has neglected to say that the German Missionary Council met in Berlin the following year, that we had a public debate in that council on it with my colleague Prof. Hollenweger and myself, that we went further and we published the main thesis of Prof. Beyerhaus in the *International Review of Mission* and a series of articles by people around the world on the subject. So that to say that it and all the rest of it has been ignored is a rather curious way of putting the issue.

And I must come back to the point I want to make to this meeting. Let us have the Frankfurt Declaration as a document like many other documents in this meeting, but I do plead with us that we do not turn this meeting into a discussion of a document that was written out of a particular situation by a particular group judging other people without a proper discussion with them and pretending to make it universal.

Thank you.

C. A Plea by Bishop D. H. Class, Stuttgart.

(From *Yesterday*, the conference newspaper in Bangkok, 3 January 1973.)

A request: I would like to plead with our friends from the Third World — please do not think that the problems tackled in the Frankfurt Declaration are exclusively a West German affair. To be sure, they may be particularly acute today in West Germany, in Scandinavia, and in the United States, but who can guarantee that very similar problems will not soon also break out elsewhere? The world has become a global village. Technology is everywhere changing the feeling for life as well as human structures of thought; and all this is happening faster than we think. And last but not least: as long as God speaks with us, no one has the right to reject the dialogue. We have to meet each other, listen to each other, learn from each other even if that means much pain and disappointment — indeed, in spite of that!

Bishop Class, Germany.

D. A Position Paper by Pastor W. Gengnagel, Stuttgart.

(From *Yesterday*, the conference newspaper in Bangkok, 5/6 January 1973.)

The Real Crisis of Mission

Not every crisis in church history is of a dogmatic nature. Behind dogmatic controversies there are often other conflicts hidden. That applies to a great extent to the so-called Frankfurt Declaration. It defends with a grim courage positions which the missionary leaders in Germany do not even attack. And it fires with all guns on positions, which (in the form in which they are stated) nobody defends. The noise of gunfire however silences the real questions.

What are the real questions behind the smoke-screen?

Those are the questions which the Frankfurt Declaration does not mention, e.g., it does not speak of the churches in Africa, Asia and Latin America, which have come out of the missionary work. It does not mention that the emergence of these churches is the real crisis for missions in the old style. It is anyhow the crisis for missionary societies in Europe. One could say that the crisis is the crisis of the success of mission, for the primary goal of these missions has been reached.

They are looking around and are asking themselves a little bit confusedly: What is left for us to do? The people behind the Frankfurt Declaration deliberately ignore these questions. They see on the contrary their glory in continuing a style of the past. They measure their success by the number of European missionaries which they send to the Third World. Whether these missionaries are welcome or not does not interest them. It is in this sense that the Frankfurt Declaration is used in Germany in order to separate the mission-minded Evangelicals from the Ecumenicals, who are striving for partnership.

That is why a discussion on the Frankfurt Declaration seems to me pointless. But it would indeed be helpful if the Conference in Bangkok could develop patterns of real partnership in mission, patterns which would lead to a real independence of the partners, patterns in which the partners are truly equal, patterns which help the partners to find their true identity.

W. Gengnagel, Basel Mission, Germany.

6. TWO MESSAGES FROM BANGKOK TO THE COUNCILS, CHURCHES, AND MISSIONS AFFILIATED WITH THE COMMISSION FOR WORLD MISSION AND EVANGELISM (CWME)

(These two documents were adopted unanimously by the General Assembly of the CWME which met in Bangkok from 9 to 12 January 1973. On 30 January 1973, Director Emilio Castro sent them to the conference participants as well as to the national and regional church councils, Christian councils, or mission councils affiliated with the CWME as the first documents of the conference. After these two documents had already appeared, the official volume with the reports, recommendations, and resolutions of the two Bangkok conferences was issued.)

A. "Letter to the Churches"

(From *Bangkok Assembly 1973*, pp. 1, 2. [Prof. Beyerhaus used a German text of this document, provided by the CWME, as the basis for his "preliminary remarks"; certain minor changes have consequently been made in the English text to bring its wording into conformity with the German text. — Trans.])

(Preliminary Remarks by P. Beyerhaus:

This document was drafted by the French Reformed pastor, Jacques Maury, in Committee F of the General Assembly and was unanimously adopted in the plenary body after a few changes.

As the most widely circulated message from the Bangkok Conference this document deserves and demands very careful study. The following observations are offered as particularly important matters in the examination of this document:

(1) The word "experience" is prominent even in the first paragraph; the talk is of "receiving" and "celebrating." The letter is thus describing the conference at Bangkok as an event of faith or salvation in relationship to world Christianity; it is the kind of event which must also be communicated to the Christian world.

(2) The "riches of ecumenical reality" and the "common Bible study" are named together as the actual well-springs of the activity at Bangkok. "All that God has done for us, where we are and as we are" has become in this report a supplementary source of revelation alongside Scripture or a new key by which to interpret Scripture.

(3) In the first of the three "results" a whole series of major Christian ideas are paraded one after another. The talk is of "the living person of Jesus Christ," the uniqueness of His name for salvation, the "work of the Holy Spirit," the "power of salvation by His cross as it is manifest in His resurrection," of the "true conversion of men and women to God," and the "conclusive revelation of His victory." This at first awakens the impression that the fundamental assertions of the Christian creed are being affirmed afresh. But under close reading it is revealed that all these formulations have been put out of joint with respect to the original biblical assertions. For example, the reference to the "power of salvation by His cross as it is manifest in His resurrection" is a typically modernistic formulation in which the essence of the power of salvation by His cross as a propitiatory sacrifice for our guilt is misconstrued and the actuality of the personal, bodily resurrection of Jesus Christ is also called into question. One is reminded of the thesis of the Bultmann school that the message of the resurrection is merely an aid to put the meaning of Jesus' death into words. Resurrection can, for example, mean just that the influence of Jesus' example of self-giving for other people continues on even after death. There is also no mention of the personal return of Christ but rather of the "conclusive revelation of His victory" which in the way these words were used by Miss Pauline Webb (cf. p. 35f.) can be exhaustively interpreted as an event of the revolutionary struggle for liberation within history. This interpretation is even suggested by the fact that such a victory is said to be visible already wherever a person as a child of God attains his "true liberty and accepts his

responsibility as a person." The goal of salvation history is thus humanization, or the process by which someone achieves freedom or personhood. The Bible, on the other hand, describes the conclusive victory of Jesus at His return as something very different than this. The apparently biblical language should not deceive people to the fact that the biblical concepts used here have been thoroughly filled by human ideology and have borrowed much from Marxist humanism.

(4) The practical program of church and missionary activity that is outlined in the second "result" shows still more clearly that the ideological interpretation of the first "result" does not miss the mark. In this second portion those guidelines that are foundational for the missionary task as given by Jesus — that is, "make disciples, preach the Gospel, baptize, forgive sins, teach" (cf. Matt. 28:19; Mark 16:15; Luke 24:47; John 20:23) — play virtually no role at all. When it comes to the sending of missionaries, there is only the negative talk of the recommended moratorium to withdraw temporarily foreign personnel and money in selected situations, and it is even stronger here than in the report of Section 3. On the other hand, a heavy emphasis was laid on the ecumenical understanding of missions that has taken the place of the biblical concepts — this was in fact the understanding with which the Bangkok Conference was almost exclusively concerned. Its major elements are the struggle against racism, against social, economic, and political oppression as well as against the Indochina War. Reference to a "spoken witness" strikes one as a mere formality; it is, moreover, immediately supplemented by a description of *dialogue* in which the non-Christian partner in the discussion is even called a brother in Christ through whom God wants to enrich us.

(5) But the most far-reaching requests of the letter are found in the third "result." The CWME desires to create new structures for a twice-named "church universal" so that we together can do justice to our common task on the six continents of a divided world. Here again confession is made of the church's world task in terms of the effort to join together in finding our "full identity" with "creative imagination." At least this is the task to fulfill once traditional patterns of mission relationships have been broken off. The letter closes by acknowledging a "great hope"; but this is a "hope" which does not in any sense coincide with the content of the biblical promise.

On the basis of thoughts such as these, the two conventions of the Conference of Confessing Communions in the Protestant Churches of Germany in their position paper 2 March 1973, on the World Mission Conference in Bangkok requested Christians "to be very critical in evaluating the reports and results from Bangkok, including the 'Letter to the Churches,' that are being spread with such great diligence and not to let themselves be deceived by the familiar biblical phrases that are used, for the true character of these publications is actually contrary to the Gospel."

In a "Reply" to this Frankfurt position paper the six official delegates of the German Protestant Missionary Council and the Protestant Board for World Mission responded with a statement drafted by the executive secretary of the German Protestant Missionary Council, P. G. Buttler: "In the warning to 'all Christians' not to let themselves be deceived by the familiar biblical phrases used in the statements and reports of Bangkok to mask a position contrary to the Gospel, we see a particularly objectionable type of slander. With unspiritual arrogance it denies the integrity of others and divides brothers who confess a common Christ as their Lord and Savior." (Protestant Press Service E.P.D. Documents of 26 March 1973, pp. 33, 34.)

The reader now has the opportunity to decide for himself whether the theological observations I have made above are on the mark or whether they are in fact a "particularly objectionable type of slander." The American critique ("Salvation Today — WCC Views — WCC Words"), given as an appendix to these two documents, will also serve as a supplementary aid in helping the reader make up his mind.)

Letter to the churches from the Bangkok Assembly: Salvation Today

Coming from all the continents of our earth we have met in Bangkok to explore together the promise and demands of Salvation Today. We have received more than we expected; we have experienced the full reality of this promise and we have celebrated it in joy and in reality. We want to share with you the experience of these days, which for two convergent reasons has been very rich.

(1) This conference, perhaps more than any previous one, has given most of us a deeper understanding of the riches of ecumenical reality. All of us, freely and in confidence of true fellowship, have been able, and have known how, to voice our own concerns, sufferings and hopes. The dialogue was frank, without compromise and challenging for the future, in particular between the poor and the rich within and between nations. We regret that the small number of Orthodox participants prevented a fuller expression of ecumenicity.

(2) We have realized the power of renewal contained in the Gospel when it is shared and read together in a common Bible study and when each one and each group can tell what it demands in his or her own situation. To make this so everyone's identity must be respected. Sharing, not only in word, but also in prayer, song and art, of all that God has done for us, where we are and as we are, has profoundly enriched us who came from Africa, the Americas, Asia, Europe and the Pacific.

From our sharing three results have become clear:

(1) Without evading or minimizing theological debates it has become clear that it is around the living person of Jesus Christ that we have met, reliving "that there is no other name given among men by which we must be saved." Through the work of the Holy Spirit we have recognized

together the power of salvation by His cross as it is manifest in His resurrection.

Thus it is to Him that we call you to turn. Beyond our own confusions, in the midst of our most complex problems, God is offering us His salvation which is simple and comprehensive, a wonderful turning upside down of the usual course of events, of our world, expressed in the true conversion of men and women to God.

We have also recognized that it is the whole of human reality that He wants to free from all that keeps it in slavery. In accepting the total weakness of the cross "All power has been given to him." Even as we wait for the conclusive revelation of His victory, we see Him victoriously at work every time a man or woman comes to true liberty and accepts His responsibility as a person — a child of God.

(2) Face to face with him whom we have also met as our judge we become aware of the sharpness of His demands and of the gap that exists between what we believe and what we do. Because of the salvation that is in Jesus Christ and which promises to all "the glorious liberty of the children of God" we commit ourselves more fully in the struggle against everything that oppresses men and women today, not only the sin that is in them but also that is in societies. The scandals of racism, of social injustices, of economic and political oppression, the tragic shame of the Indochina war or the bloody suppression of liberation movements, the dehumanization of technological civilization and the threat that it poses for the future of humanity, all these challenge Christians urgently to express in action the salvation of Jesus Christ.

This necessary obedience to the liberating power of Christ, in a coherence of faith and life, must be accompanied by analysis of the situations where it is to be carried out. The abusive misuse of all kinds of power, including the compromise of the churches in this area, must be frankly seen and clearly denounced.

The cross of Christ where His love went to the bitter end forces us to recognize how often we stop along the road and impells us to start walking joyously even if the path leads to sacrifice. It compels us to engage in spoken witness and to enter into dialogue with all those, of one faith or another, of one conviction or another, who also are loved by God. In spite of differences, the other must never be regarded as an enemy, but through Jesus Christ as a brother or sister through whom God wants to enrich us.

(3) The experience of sharing in Bangkok obliges us to keep on searching for structures of a common life that will enrich our lives. It is clear that we must find new ways of responding together to our common calling to mission in the six continents of one divided world, so that everyone may take full responsibility and obtain full identity. In this respect we are only at the beginning of the road. We have however noted the development of some promising experiments which call us all to use more creative

imagination to find a mature and honest relationship. For this to be a true renewal we shall be led to make some painful decisions. So that the full and responsible identity of the traditionally receiving churches may be more speedily furthered, it may be necessary to have a temporary withdrawal of foreign funds and personnel.

It is at the local level that the reality of the church universal must be lived. In today's world with an ever-growing migration which challenges our communities, all of our churches are called to receive the strangers in their midst as brothers and sisters who manifest the reality of the church universal and share in its local mission. God has set before us riches that we must learn to receive.

It is under the sign of great hope that we write. In the humility to which we are forced by our powerlessness we have learned once again that "the word of God is not bound" and that it opens wide the doors of salvation.

B. "Affirmation on Salvation Today." (A Confession of Faith)

(From *Bangkok Assembly 1973*, pp. 42, 43.)

(Preliminary Remarks by P. Beyerhaus:

This document in its original text arose as the product of Bible Study Group 3 in the first days of the World Conference on "Salvation Today." The joint authors were Arthur Glasser, Professor of Missiology at Fuller Theological Seminary and an evangelical, and Mr. Edward H. Johnson from the Presbyterian Church in Canada. In this Bible study group a particularly conservative circle had been brought together. The Affirmation appeared first in the conference newspaper, *Yesterday*, on 5/6 January 1973, p. 5, and was then, after a few changes by the General Assembly, unanimously adopted at the close of the whole conference. The traditionally evangelical tone of this document created some disquiet among the conference leadership as is clear from the remarks of Dr. G. Hoffmann concerning it [cf. p. 81f. of this book]. Even Director Emilio Castro, who sent out this document together with the "Letter to the Churches," expressed the opinion in his covering letter that this affirmation did not bear a dogmatically binding character but was only to be understood as a personal testimony of experience: "It is not to be a confession of faith but an expression of a common persuasion by the participants at the Bangkok Conference that they should share their common experiences with us: a challenge not only to widen our own understanding of salvation but truly to live with its power." It was consequently not included in the official German report on the Bangkok Conference, edited by Prof. Potter.

But in fact even this evangelical document was permeated by certain ideological assertions [italicized in the text] which incorporate it as well into the general ecumenical atmosphere of the conference.)

Affirmation on Salvation Today

As we have met together in this fellowship,
we have experienced the joy of the living Christ
and have been renewed and challenged
by the mutual faith one of another.

We have been deeply conscious of our failures
in obedience to our Lord
and our blindness to the ways He sets before us.
We are moved by a profound feeling of penitence
which both pains us
and frees us for Christ's renewal.

Over and above our distress
at the problems and perplexities of the world,
and our confusion about the structures and role of the church
we see the shining of the Light
which no darkness can quench.

With gratitude and joy we affirm again
our confidence in the sufficiency of our crucified and risen Lord.
We know Him as the One who is, who was and who is to come,
the sovereign Lord of all.

To the individual He comes with power
to liberate him from every evil and sin,
from every power in heaven and earth,
and from every threat of life or death.

To the world He comes as the Lord of the universe,
with deep compassion for the poor and the hungry,
to liberate the powerless and the oppressed.
To the powerful and the oppressors He comes
in judgment and mercy.

We see God at work today
both within the church and beyond the church
toward the achievement of his purpose
that justice might shine on every nation.

He calls His church to be part of His saving activity
both in calling men to decisive personal response to His Lordship
and in unequivocal commitment to the movements and works
by which all men may know justice
and have opportunity to be fully human.

In joyous trust in Christ's power and victory
we can live with freedom and hope
whatever the present may be.

The Lord is at hand.

Supplement: An American Critique

(From a lead article in *American Church News*, the official organ of the
"Church Union," a confessional fellowship within the Protestant Episcopal
Church in the United States, vol. 37, no. 10 [1973], p. 4.)

(Preliminary Remarks by P. Beyerhaus:

In light of the observations contained in our introductory comments
concerning the ambiguous theological language of the "Letter to the
Churches" and the "Affirmation on Salvation Today," it is most interesting
that an American ecclesiastical journal has come to a similar conclusion.
Indeed it gives an even more radically ideological interpretation of the
biblical concepts that are used in modern ecumenical pronouncements.
This lead article [anonymous] in the *American Church News* was in the
issue devoted essentially to the Bangkok Conference. The consistently
Marxist interpretations which the author feels ecumenical statements have
given to certain basic Christian concepts do frequently seem a bit extreme,
and, given the pluralistic nature of ecumenical meetings, they certainly do
not strike home in every instance; nevertheless, the article does aid us to
keep listening closely to the ambiguous character of such language and to be
aware of the ideological pitfalls latent in it. It also keeps us from being
easily moved from our traditional understanding of these central biblical
concepts to an approval of such documents. And at the very least, it draws
our attention to the fact that the same texts can be interpreted and also
judged practically in completely different ways by different authors and
readers, each according to the theological or ideological presuppositions by
which they themselves are guided.

The truly seductive danger in our present situation — ecclesiastical, theological, and also ecumenical — lies precisely in this ambiguous use of
Christian language.)

"Salvation Today" — WCC Views — WCC Words

Religion as you have known it is an illusion, an opiate to hold you in
subjection to an oppressive system. The World Council offers you power
and identity and the things of this world. But for this you must give up the
illusion that you are a person with a soul that God wishes to save for a
divine purpose. Your time on earth is the only life you will ever have. You
are a creature of your world; outside of your identity as social categories —
your class, your race, your nation, your community — you do not exist.

Since it is your social structures that are the reality that creates you, it is they that are oppressive and unjust — *Sinful*. Therefore, it is not you that needs saving but your society. You must create new structures to give you self-realization, power, identity and wealth — *Salvation*. To accomplish this you must empower your identifying categories — class, nation, race — *The Elect*. Science tells us that power is a function of applied force; therefore, force must be applied to all of the tensions in society in order to polarize them to the breaking point — *Mission*. This proceeds by all possible methods from the "dripping water" technique of dialectical dialogue — *Evangelism*, all the way up to the violent cataclysm of "dialectical liberation" — *Exodus Model*. We will then create for you a society in which you are powerful, wealthy and realized — *Eschatology*.

Note carefully that the chief enemy of mankind lies in the western world and in the western Church. Because the Christian Church is corrupt and a captive in the service of the oppressive and exploiting societies, it must die — *Crucifixion*. Its life will be sacrificed as a means to power in the service of revolution — *Atonement*. Thus will be assuaged the guilt of its complicity in injustice — *Repentance*. As a believing Christian, you must repress oppression and oppose structures of violence with violence — *Agape*.

Since your doctrines, theologies, liturgies, ministries and missions are expressive of an unjust and oppressive social order, they must be syncretized out of all meaning or transmuted into polarizing instruments for the dialectical transfiguration of society. As Dr. Philip Potter, the WCC Secretary General, has stated at Bangkok, a proclamation-centered evangelism is a heresy — *Renewal*.

Since salvation is a dialectical historical process leading to the perfection of social structures for all mankind, no one can be saved until all men are saved. But here the visions of Karl Marx were unfortunately murky as regards paradise. This may delay your salvation. However, we as the peoples' guardian of their liberation will see that they stay conformed at any sacrifice to the inevitable principles of historical development and social change — *Ministry*. As history unfolds within the iron law of cause and effect (dialectical materialism), you can look forward, under our creative direction, to a state of permanent revolution — *Eternal Bliss*. You will have become psycho-socio-historically evolved; you are no longer a person, you are now an intersection of categories — *Paradise*.

7. EXCERPTS FROM THE SECTION REPORTS OF THE WORLD CONFERENCE ON "SALVATION TODAY" FROM 29 DECEMBER 1972, to 8 JANUARY 1973

(The following material presents some extracts from the reports of the three sections and their ten subsections which met from 2-6 January 1973.)

A. From Section 1, "Culture and Identity"

The report of this section was divided as follows:

(I) On Racial Identity

(*Bangkok Assembly 1973*, p. 75f.)

• • •

(7) *An interpretation of "Black Theology"*

• • •

(d) The Incarnation took place in a particular context: Jesus was born a Jew, as a member of a particular race. Yet it has universal meaning: Jesus came to save the world. Therefore the Son of God comes into the history of every people when in the Incarnation He becomes a member of their own family. Hence He is identified among "black" people as the oppressed one.

The universality of the Christian faith does not contradict its particularity. Christ has to be responded to in a particular situation. Many people try to give universal validity to their own particular response instead of acknowledging that the diversity of responses to Christ is essential precisely because they are related to particular situations and are thus relevant and complementary. One such response is explicated in Black Theology.

(e) Black theology shocks many Christians. Yet it exposes traditional white theology (e.g., American, British, German, etc.) which they accept without qualms. This is because the West has arrogated to itself the right to determine the criteria for what is acceptable or not acceptable in all spheres of human endeavor. Black theology shocks because it repudiates this arrogant claim.

Proper theology includes reflection on the experience of the Christian community in a particular place, at a particular time. Thus, it will be necessarily a contextual theology; it will be a relevant and living theology which refuses to be easily universalized because it speaks to and out of a particular situation.

Black theology tries to make sense of the particular black experience of suffering and oppression from rampant white racism, in the light of God's revelation in Jesus Christ. It is a theology of liberation and, as such, is really a theology of the oppressed, so that it may legitimately be appropriated by those who are dehumanized by oppression whatever the color of their skin. It affirms the personhood of the oppressed and asserts that God offers them salvation in Jesus Christ as the persons for whom Christ died, proclaiming that they do not need to apologize for their existence. They are God's children as blacks or whatever. Christ is their brother who shares their whole life because He places Himself unequivocally on the side of the oppressed and the powerless. . . .

(IV) On Dialogue With People of Living Faiths

(*Bangkok Assembly 1973*, pp. 78-80.)

(1) Meeting in Thailand provided opportunities for the experience of dialogue, in visits to a nearby Buddhist monastery, listening to a senior Buddhist monk explaining the Buddhist way of meditation, meeting with monks and laymen who explained their faith and life. We learned something of the social and political conditions of this country and heard from the local Christian Church of a growing questioning among people in Bangkok about the meaninglessness of life for many, and their search for something deeper, indeed for a new identity. Because of the rare opportunity we had to meet Buddhists in their own environment, both religious and social, we felt that it was appropriate to give more time to this matter and to commend the question of ideologies for study at a later meeting.

(2) It was clear from members of the section that dialogue is taking place in many parts of the world, under greatly varying conditions, and with differing degrees of intensity and effectiveness. The need to listen in order to understand and communicate was acknowledged. Members of the group testified to their own experience of the clarification of the Christian faith and the crystallization of expression resulting from the questioning and probing of their partner in dialogue.

(3) The call to dialogue arises out of our faith: the affirmation of salvation in Jesus Christ in all its aspects of forgiveness, liberation from injustice and oppression, fulfillment in personal and community life and the development of an inner spiritual life, is our starting point. Although often inadequately interpreted by Christians and misunderstood by others, the cross of Christ and the vindication of this in the resurrection, are central. Christians cannot but be faithful to this and more urgently so as they experience these facts in their own life.

(4) We are conscious of God's movement toward men both as Creator and Savior, bringing man to wholeness and leading him to wider community. We see in the Bible the record of His saving acts among the people of the Sinai covenant, in the incarnate life of our Lord and in the world mission given to the Church. Our eyes will be keenly open to discover what He is doing among people of other faiths.

(5) Reciprocally, in dialogue adherents of other living faiths speak out of their own experience. We are called to listen carefully to the insights by which they live and the effects in character, daily living and community spirit of these insights. This implies that they, too, have a mission.

(6) We are involved in dialogue as we share common human aspirations and responsibilities with our fellow men. In dialogue with people of living faiths we meet persons who are formed by specific religious and cultural traditions and claim an authentic relationship with the Ultimate, which they acknowledge. We must recognize our partners as they perceive and experience their existence and the world as religious persons committed to a definite faith. They share in dialogue from this starting point as we are called from our commitment to Christ, grateful for what He has done for us and for others, for His love for the world and His desire that all men shall be saved and come to know the truth (1 Tim. 2:4).

(7) We would be as eager to listen as to speak. Indeed we know that we shall not be able to communicate effectively unless we listen. Our dialogue will be open and free, with a readiness to probe and to be probed. We shall rejoice in the common ground we discover, we shall be equally eager to discover our differences, some of which may be resolved when we understand the spiritual, experiential and conceptual background from which others start and the difficulty of language. As to apparently irreconcilable differences we shall remember our Lord's promise that the Spirit will lead us into all truth (John 16:13).

(8) In our discussion we considered the relationship between dialogue and evangelism. Is there an inescapable tension between them as some fear? This is not necessarily so. We will be faithful to our Lord's command to mission and witness, which is part of our title deed and which people of other faiths know as a duty for Christians as their own faith-relationship with the Ultimate gives them a sense of universal significance. A desire to share and a readiness to let others share with us should inspire our witness to Christ rather than a desire to win a theological argument. We were glad to note that increasingly mission is being carried on in this spirit of dialogue without the subsequent decrease in the sense of urgency in evangelism.

(9) It is hardly necessary to point out that we live in pluralistic societies. People of different faiths move about the world to live and work in other countries. There are missionary activities of religions in lands outside their countries of origin and tradition. At the same time there is a universal search for a new identity. Because of this reciprocal mission, Christian world mission may once more become acceptable as an authentic expression of Christian faith and not be open to the charge of religious imperialism. The resulting confrontation and dialogue will lead to deeper understanding, the clearing away of ignorance about each other and a sharpening of the imperative of commitment.

(10) As the interdependence between people and nations is increasing, there is a manifest need for world community. As people of different living faiths and ideological persuasions we are all confronted with this need. It is in this light that all are challenged to understand afresh the universal significance of their faith. Christians can gladly work with others to meet

human needs, relieve human suffering, establish social justice, work for wider community and struggle for peace. In this connection it may be worth noting that the theme of world community has appeared again and again in dialogue with people of living faiths. This common search needs to be pursued.

(11) We have already said that our attitude to people of other faiths arises out of our understanding of God's will that all men shall be saved. Therefore we urge our member churches to go forward with eager faith, with greater love for our fellowmen, with prayer for guidance and with confidence that God is at work among all people to make His saving love available for all in every generation and to build the kingdom of His love, which we Christians see manifested in Jesus Christ.

(V) Some Meditations

(*Bangkok Assembly 1973*, pp. 80, 83.)

Lord, show us deeply how important it is to be useless. . . .

It was the drug scene, you were lost and wretched, and you put your hand in the hand of the Man who calmed the sea.
                                        I rejoice with you, my sister.

You are turned on by the exciting and ever-deepening insights of Scripture.
                                        I rejoice with you, my brother.

You were converted from shallowness to mystic depths through discipline and meditation.
                                        I rejoice with you, my sister.

You were a poor Mexican baptized by the Holy Spirit and the Blood of the Lamb.
                                        I rejoice with you, my brother.

You were an intellectual Chinese who broke through the barrier between yourself and the dung-smelling peasant.
                                        I rejoice with you, my sister.

You found all the traditional language meaningless and became "an atheist by the grace of God."
                                        I rejoice with you, my brother.

Out of the depths of your despair and bondage you cried and in your cry was poignant hope.
                                        I rejoice with you, my sister.

You were oppressed and fled to the liberated area and dedicated your life to revolutionary struggle.
                                        I rejoice with you, my brother.

You were oppressed and put down by male authority and in spite of sneers and snarls persevered in your quest for dignity.

I rejoice with you, my sister.

For all my brothers and sisters who have entered the struggle for social and spiritual liberation — I rejoice.

Victory and grace be unto you.

(VI) Recommendations

(*Bangkok Assembly 1973, p. 85.*)

(1) Considering the concrete situation of people living in Africa under Portuguese colonialism, we as Christians declare that colonial domination is anti-Christian because it denies to each man his inalienable right to personhood. No church can support such a system without betraying her own vocation and mission in the world. We therefore call on the WCME Assembly in Bangkok and the WCC Executive in Bangalore to urge its member churches:

(a) To give maximum publicity to the true state of affairs in the Portuguese colonies and for church leaders to refuse to go on good will tours to these countries.

(b) To send a widely representative delegation to the liberated areas to report on the real situation there.

(c) To launch a campaign to increase aid through the Program to Combat Racism for the educational, social and medical work of the liberation movements and to provide the means of delivering such aid to the liberated areas.

(d) To urge missionary agencies to examine critically their identity as part of the colonial power structures and their involvement through finance and personnel.

(e) To mobilize public opinion in favor of the legitimacy of the struggle of oppressed people for their liberation.

(2)

(a) That in their preaching and teaching ministry churches in areas of colonial and racial domination should awaken in people the consciousness of their cultural identity and continually help them to affirm their personhood.

(b) That in future strategy patterns of missionary engagement that reflect cultural imperialism be abandoned by churches and mission agencies.

B. From Section 2, "Salvation and Social Justice."

(*Bangkok Assembly 1973*, pp. 87-97.)

Introduction

The task of Section 2 was to consider the relationship of God's action for salvation to the world-wide struggles for social justice. In presenting our report we would stress that we recognize the work of Section II as an integral part of the total discussion of Salvation Today. Our concentration upon the social, economic and political implications of the Gospel does not in any way deny the personal and eternal dimensions of salvation. Rather, we would emphasize that the personal, social, individual and corporate aspects of salvation are so interrelated that they are inseparable. . . .

The guidelines which came out of the discussion of these action reports are presented in the form of the recommendations which follow.

The theological reflections which came out of our discussions both in plenary session and the subsections have been brought together into the statement entitled "Salvation and Social Justice Within a Divided Humanity" with which we begin our Section's report to this conference.

(I) Salvation and Social Justice in a Divided Humanity

(A) *The Mission of God*

In the power of the Spirit Christ is sent from God the Father into this divided world "to preach the Gospel to the poor, to heal the brokenhearted, to preach deliverance to the captives and recovering of sight to the blind, to set at liberty the oppressed, and to proclaim the year of God's favor" (Luke 4:18). Through Christ men and women are liberated and empowered with all their energies and possibilities to participate in His Messianic work. Through His death on the cross and His resurrection from the dead hope of salvation becomes realistic and reality hopeful. He liberates from the prison of guilt. He takes the inevitability out of history. In Him the kingdom of God and of free people is at hand. Faith in Christ releases in man creative freedom for the salvation of the world. He who separates Himself from the mission of God separates Himself from salvation.

The salvation which Christ brought, and in which we participate, offers a comprehensive wholeness in this divided life. We understand salvation as newness of life — the unfolding of true humanity in the fullness of God (Col. 2:9). It is salvation of the soul and the body, of the individual and society, mankind and "the groaning creation" (Rom. 8:19). As evil works both in personal life and in exploitative social structures which humiliate humankind, so God's justice manifests itself both in the justification of the sinner and in social and political justice.

As guilt is both individual and corporate so God's liberating power changes both persons and structures. We have to overcome the dichotomies in our thinking between soul and body, person and society, human kind and creation. Therefore we see the struggles for economic justice, political freedom and cultural renewal as elements in the total liberation of the world through the mission of God. This liberation is finally fulfilled when "death is swallowed up in victory" (1 Cor. 15:55). This comprehensive notion of salvation demands of the whole of the people of God a matching comprehensive approach to their participation in salvation.

(B) *Salvation and Liberation of Churches and Christians*

Many Christians who for Christ's sake are involved in economic and political struggles against injustice and oppression ask themselves and the churches what it means today to be a Christian and a true church. Without the salvation of the churches from their captivity in the interests of dominating classes, races and nations, there can be no saving church. Without liberation of the churches and Christians from their complicity with structural injustice and violence, there can be no liberating church for mankind. Every church, all Christians, face the question whether they serve Christ and His saving work alone, or at the same time also the powers of inhumanity. "No man can serve two masters, God and mammon" (Matt. 6:24). We must confess our misuse of the name of Christ by the accommodation of the churches to oppressive powers, by our self-interested apathy, lovelessness, and fear. We are seeking the true community of Christ which works and suffers for His kingdom. We seek the charismatic church which activates energies for salvation (1 Cor. 12). We seek the church which initiates actions for liberation and supports the work of other liberating groups without calculating self-interest. We seek a church which is the catalyst of God's saving work in the world, a church which is not merely the refuge of the saved but a community serving the world in the love of Christ.

(C) *Salvation in Four Dimensions*

Within the comprehensive notion of salvation, we see the saving work in four social dimensions:

(1) Salvation works in the struggle for economic justice against the exploitation of people by people.

(2) Salvation works in the struggle for human dignity against political oppression of human beings by their fellow men.

(3) Salvation works in the struggle for solidarity against the alienation of person from person.

(4) Salvation works in the struggle of hope against despair in personal life.

In the process of salvation, we must relate these four dimensions to each other. There is no economic justice without political freedom, no political freedom without economic justice. There is no social justice without solidarity, no solidarity without social justice. There is no justice, no human dignity, no solidarity without hope, no hope without justice, dignity and solidarity. But there are historical priorities according to which salvation is anticipated in one dimension first, be it the personal, the political or the economic dimension. These points of entry differ from situation to situation in which we work and suffer. We should know that such anticipations are not the whole of salvation, and must keep in mind the other dimensions while we work. Forgetting this denies the wholeness of salvation. Nobody can do in any particular situation everything at the same time. There are various gifts and tasks, but there is one spirit and one goal. In this sense, it can be said, for example, that salvation is the peace of the people in Vietnam, independence in Angola, justice and reconciliation in Northern Ireland and release from the captivity of power in the North Atlantic community, or personal conversion is the release of a submerged society into hope, or of new life styles amidst corporate self-interest and lovelessness.

(D) Means and Criteria of Saving Work

Speaking of salvation realistically, we cannot avoid the question of proper means. The means are different in the four dimensions referred to. We will produce no economic justice without participation in, and use of, economic power. We will win no political freedom without participation, and discriminating use of, political power. We cannot overcome cultural alienation without the use of cultural influence. In this framework we discussed the physical use of liberating violence against oppressive violence. The Christian tradition is ambiguous on this question because it provides no justification of violence and no rejection of political power. Jesus' commandment to love one's enemy presupposes enmity. One should not become the enemy of one's enemy, but should liberate him from his enmity (Matt. 5:43-48). This commandment warns against the brutality of violence and reckless disregard of life. But in the cases of institutionalized violence, structural injustice and legalized immorality, love also involves the right of resistance and the duty "to repress tyranny" (Scottish Confession) with responsible choice among the possibilities we have. One then may become guilty for love's sake, but can trust in the forgiveness of guilt. Realistic work for salvation proceeds through confrontation, but depends, everywhere and always, on reconciliation with God.

(II) Subsection A — Recommendations

(A) A response to the question

"Should a foreign mission agency withdraw from an unjust situation where the majority is being dominated by a powerful minority? What considerations are relevant to this discussion?"

Some Criteria Proposed as Possible Guidelines

(1) Each case is unique and complex, and requires special concrete consideration. There is no universal formula.

(2) A commitment to justice as a top priority on the part of the mission agency working in such situations is seen as essential.

(3) Mission under these conditions should be conceived of particularly in terms of what is required in obedience to Christ the liberator. This means an assessment of the political significance of remaining or withdrawing, and the likely impact of either course of action on issues of human dignity and freedom. . . .

(7) If the mission agency is to remain in the situation, or withdraw, is it in either case actively using its resources (money, personnel, leverage, education) and its freedom of action in its own country in such a way as to seek consciously to undermine oppression and foster liberation in the oppressive situation? The investment issue, political action, economic strategies, making the church and country aware in a variety of ways, comes in here if there is to be validation of mission to an oppressed people. . . .

(11) How does the presence of missionaries relate to the total human situation of the oppressed people? Are they able to serve the whole community, or just the Christians? Are they providing services to all the people of the area in the name of the church (medical, educational, community development) which would be eliminated if they left (as in Angola), thus depriving people of some elements of a fully human life which inheres in the church's liberating mission? . . .

(13) What is the attitude of liberation movements where they exist, as in relation to Southern African countries? Has there been consultation with them, concerning a total strategy for the welfare of the oppressed people in the country? And what is likely to be the consequence of a decision to remain or withdraw, for the long-range future of the church following independence? And are the agencies committed to political liberation?

(14) Is there a policy of careful selection and orientation of missionaries working in situations of great injustice, so that they can understand the complexities involved and be committed with integrity and sensitivity to Christ's liberating mission, and in such a way as not to bring further suffering upon church and people? . . .

(III) Subsection B — Economic Exploitation

The theme of our subsection forced us to reconsider the concept of power and powerlessness. We realized that this field was seriously neglected by churches and missions and that they often were guilty of accepting the status quo.

166

Latin America's exploitation by the USA and the action model in the Netherlands (X-Y movement) involving awareness, political pressure and self-taxation were examples of how on the one hand rich countries misuse their power and on the other hand a movement enables people to become involved in the process of liberation.

In the discussion it often was asserted that mission expansion was closely related to the exploitative nature of the capitalist system. Even today many of our missionary and evangelistic efforts are exclusively concerned about individual salvation and remain unwilling to deal with the causes of social injustice.

We were disturbed about the false dichotomies which influence missionary theology and methods: the body-spirit, the individual-corporate dichotomies. There is a need for a rediscovery of the biblical dimension of the Gospel in terms of freedom, justice and grace. The Gospel always relates to man in his totality. The Gospel is therefore a liberating power over oppressive powers, which makes even powerless people powerful. The powerlessness of Christ on the cross must be seen in the context of His liberating power over death and suffering.

We are therefore making the following recommendations to the CWME Assembly:

(1) to promote and support self-taxation of individuals and churches everywhere as an expression of transfer of power from the powerful to the powerless;

(2) to expose the negative influence of the "donor mentality" manifested in development aid ("help-syndrome") thus perpetuating existing economic and political systems. . . .

(V) Subsection D — Local Struggles

(A) *Setting and Issues*

(1) We were asked to deal with two action reports — Centro Sviluppo 2 (Sicily) and Zone One Tondo Organization (Manila). However, we also received and considered additional action reports from Paraguay and India. Whereas ZOTO is a people's organization among the urban poor in Manila representing about 100 people's organizations with 80,000 members, Centro Sviluppo 2 is a farming commune in rural Sicily. Cases in Paraguay and India were brought from rural areas. All were concerned with action in a local situation.

(2) In the four major areas covered the issue of land was most important. It was asserted that the poor, urban and rural, have a common oppressor in the capitalistic system that monopolizes and exploits the land. Private ownership in urban areas and feudalistic control of land in rural areas deny the poor any possibility of achieving their manhood.

(3) Legality of action was questioned seriously. Any action for change would encounter with questions of law and order. It is more so when the power legalizes the immorality and violates basic human rights. Struggles of the poor and the powerless will then be seeking a broader basis of legitimacy of their action. Where injustice is sanctioned by law and when the exploiting system is imposed by it even an illegal action should be sought on the basis of human rights and general consensus of the oppressed.

(4) Although the importance of local struggle ought to be emphasized the national and international dimension of issue(s) should not be overlooked. Actions based on concrete local scenes are essential for substantial and meaningful change. Local actions, however, should not be isolated from others, as the systems and structures which cause suffering of the people are either nationally or internationally interwoven.

(5) The group felt also that it is too arbitrary to divide our mission along geographical lines only, e.g., urban and rural. Empowering the poor and the powerless should be stressed equally both in urban slums and among the rural poor.

(B) Methodology

(1) In every instance the primary concern was for the awareness of the dispossessed masses. It is a program which educates and informs the people about the meaning and cause of the situation and what they can and must do about it. It is the people themselves who are the best advocates of themselves.

(2) In relation with the awareness, techniques and methods of organizing the poor were felt to be important and essential for empowering the powerless. We discovered variety here, ZOTO in Manila has been established with a strong organization reflecting a democratic organization of the people. In Sicily a group of people has organized a farm commune and through it they are carrying on a program of awareness, providing a model for a neighboring community. In Paraguay, this process is carried on through church auspices.

(3) It was recognized that it is essential to establish a coalition of all other agencies concerned in the community for more effective action. . . .

3. From Section III, Churches Renewed in Mission."

(Bangkok Assembly 1973, pp. 102-106.)

•   •   •

Subsection III B: Growing Churches and Renewal

•   •   •

(C) Relationship between the growth of the church and salvation of mankind.

Salvation is Jesus Christ's liberation of individuals from sin and all its consequences. It also is a task which Jesus Christ accomplishes through His church to free the world from all forms of oppression. This can happen only if the church is renewed and grows.

(1) Each generation must evangelize its own generation. To work for *church growth and renewal* is the chief abiding and irreplaceable task of Christian mission.

(2) The church may grow in number and in doctrinal understanding, but may lack an awareness of the call of Christ to participate with Him in liberating society.

(3) The church may deepen its spiritual life and develop its social services, but may still not hear the call of Christ to pass on His invitation, to those who do not know Him, to be reconciled to God.

(4) All institutions which have made an impact on the world in the past and are doing so today (whether in evangelism, church planting, social service, or the struggle for justice) have been uniformly characterized by an exclusive absorption in their objective, total devotion, and a discipline without which they never would have succeeded. This characterized the apostles as well as all missionary orders and religious societies that have enabled the church to perform her mission in the world. All experienced conflict. All had to embrace the cross and pay the price of suffering (Col. 1:24) to succeed.

(5) The world-wide church represents a diversity of spiritual experiences, theological traditions, cultural perspectives and historical experiences. However, *unity* must be expressed; this is of the essence of mission. *Diversity* in structural expression and objectives is essential to our renewal and growth. We accept this *diversity* in *unity* which we have in Christ.

(D) Our mission

At the end of the report, and in conclusion, we would like to state what seemed to us to be the central fact in all our reflections: to know what is the aim of our mission.

It is our mission

— to call men to God's salvation in Jesus Christ.

— to help them to grow in faith and in their knowledge of Christ in whom God reveals and restores to us our true humanity, our identity as men and women created in His image.

— to invite them to let themselves be constantly recreated in this image, in an eschatological community which is committed to man's struggle for liberation, unity, justice, peace and the fullness of life.

(E) Recommendations

(1) To the Assembly of CWME:

In view of the importance of the things which we have learned during this Conference for the future of the churches, we recommend that the Assembly:

— take all necessary measures to enable the church to share with us in what we have received;

— recognize that the Conference at Bangkok must not be the end of study of "Salvation Today." The work that was begun must continue on the level of the local churches. We have been called to march toward renewal. . . .

Subsection III C: Churches in Relationship

(A) By way of principles

(1) The issues we are dealing with are not new. We are working on an old agenda about which much has been said but too little has been done. We could produce a fine report by simply lifting paragraphs from the reports of previous world and regional meetings. Our basic problem is how to break free from the frustrating cycle of repeated statements which are received, filed and not acted upon.

(2) "Partnership in mission" remains an empty slogan. Even where autonomy and equal partnership have been achieved in a formal sense, the actual dynamics are such as to perpetuate relationships of domination and dependence.

(3) The power relationships between mission agenices in Europe, North America and Australasia and the churches in other areas to which they relate, reflect the economic inequalities between the nations concerned. This is one reason — though not the primary one — why mission agencies must see the struggle for international economic justice as one of their urgent tasks today. . . .

(8) A church which is the bearer of a gospel of liberation to others must first be liberated from all that hinders its true self-expression or robs it of true sense of its own responsibility. Salvation Today in this context means the liberation of churches to be their authentic selves in mission in their own milieu.

(9) It is not only the traditionally receiving churches that need this liberation. Sending churches are equally in need of it. Each church has a responsibility to help the other toward a full realization of liberty in Christ.

(10) We have considered some of the ways in which existing structures and patterns of relationship militate against the self-realization of the people of God in mission. Sometimes a pattern which alleviates one prob-

lem aggravates another. In some countries a number of churches and their mission agencies have set up an interchurch structure through which they relate in common to a church or churches in another country. This makes possible an ecumenical approach to mission on one side. However, the power of several churches thus concentrated brings undue pressure to bear on the partner church. Often such bodies take unilateral actions without adequate consultation with other bodies affected by them. Sometimes they draw one church in a given country into relationship with themselves without consulting other churches in the area, whether through the Christian Council or through other means, as to the implications of such a relationship for the cooperation of all the churches in the area in mission. . . .

(13) We also have examined more radical solutions, such as the recent proposal for a moratorium in the sending of funds and personnel for a set period of time. The whole debate on the moratorium springs from our failure to relate to one another in a way which does not dehumanize. The moratorium would enable the receiving church to find its identity, set its own priorities and discover within its own fellowship the resources to carry out its authentic mission. It would also enable the sending church to rediscover its identity in the context of the contemporary situation.

(14) It is not proposed that the moratorium be applied in every country. Missionary policy should be adapted to the particular circumstances in each area. In some parts of the world other alternatives to bilateralism should be considered. In devising new strategies for mission it is essential that all partners look together at the total challenge to mission. Churches which have been preoccupied with their bilateral relationships may find new areas for common action.

(15) In some situations, however, the moratorium proposal, painful though it may be for both sides, may be the best means of resolving a present dilemma and advancing the mission of Christ.

(B) *Recommendations*

We recommend that the Commission:

(1) Call on the mission agencies, through its affiliated councils and churches, to restructure themselves in such a way as to provide for a mature relationship with the partner churches, and to involve the latter in the process of restructuring. Such involvement will require drastic rethinking and concrete steps by all partners concerned.

(2) Urge all churches and mission agencies to review their bilateral relationships in the light of the fellowship of churches on the national and regional levels with a view to strengthening their ecumenical relationships in mission.

(3) Work with regional conferences, sponsored agencies and mission

agencies to implement the internationalization of personnel on the regional level, particularly in the field of theological education.

(4) Seek to provide for the widest possible study and discussion of the call for moratorium as a possible strategy of mission in certain areas. . . .

Addendum II, Prof. Peter Beyerhaus

(*Bangkok Assembly 1973*, pp. 108-111)

(Preliminary remarks by Prof. Beyerhaus: The report from Section III was originally to be accompanied by a theological preamble. The rector of the liberal Union Theological Seminary in Manila, Dr. Nacpil, had been assigned the task of writing it. But when he canceled his attendance on short notice, the section chairman U Kyaw Than assigned the Japanese Dr. K. Koyama, although he was not even a member of Section III but had only appeared once in a panel discussion with John Gatu and myself, along with Gatu and me to furnish a theological statement. Since, however, the draft of the preamble by Koyama could not be discussed in the section due to a lack of time, Dr. Nababan proposed that all three statements from our panel discussion be attached to the section report as addenda for which the authors were responsible. Nababan's proposal was approved in a plenary meeting of the section. This surprising decision by Section III was one of the few truly spontaneous events during the conference; it upset the strategy of our Burmese chairman which had otherwise run so well! Thus it came about that without any planning at all, my statement on the theme "Growing Churches and Renewal," which had such a completely different theological orientation, succeeded in appearing in the Bangkok Report.

In the section report, then, are found Addendum I by Kosaki Koyama, "The Identity of the Church"; Addendum III by John Gatu, "Churches Renewed in Mission"; and Addendum II, my statement that is printed here.)

Growing Churches and Renewal

An Indian village church leader once received a delegation from another Hindu village. These people were asking for a catechist to give them baptismal instruction. When the minister inquired from the messengers for what reasons they wanted to become Christians, they replied: "*Christians are different from other people.*"

In our subsection III B we considered the theme "Growing Churches and Renewal." The question as I understand it is: How far is the renewal of life a necessary precondition for the growth of the church? One could however also interpret the theme by another question: In what way do growing churches contribute to the renewal of society? Some people today think that these two questions are identical. I believe that they must be distinguished, although they are interrelated.

I

In order to answer these two questions, we have first to define what we mean by a *growing church*. The majority of action reports which we received seem to indicate that the theme basically refers to numerical growth. In recent years this concept has become a bone of contention. On the one hand there are those evangelical missions who see in numerical growth the main target. They would make church growth the chief criterion in evaluating the success of a mission. But there are others who believe that concern for numerical growth can be the expression of self-centeredness and seeking influence. I think that this is an unnecessary controversy. It is true that all good things can be done for wrong motivations, and it is even possible that a so-called growing church is not even a true church at all. But the New Testament concept of mission clearly indicates that churches are planted in view of growing numerically and that this is the way in which the largest possible number of people is saved, that is, vitally related to Jesus Christ as their Savior from sin, demonic captivity and death. The New Testament at several places directly mentions numerical growth as a real concern and cause of thanksgiving. In view of the described conflict, I think this conference should not be concluded without unequivocally reaffirming what Uppsala Section II only stated by way of admisison: that it is definitely our aim in Christian mission to work toward the growth of the church and thereby secure the salvation of man today.

But one of our action reports was about a church which is not increasing but shrinking in numbers, the church in East Germany. This made us aware that there is also another valid biblical concept of growth, namely growth in terms of spiritual maturity. Here again the New Testament clearly expresses its concern for the growth from an infant stage toward the age of manhood and perfection. In this understanding we actually could equate the terms growth and renewal. Such a growth in spiritual quality might well become the starting point for subsequent numerical growth. But this is not certain, for we know that there will be a time in history when the church is not growing numerically at all any more, as she then is entering into the period of her final testing which will be marked by the apostasy of many of her members.

II

Having discussed the nature and the desirability of a growing church, I now want to proceed to give a description of *renewal*. I shall first discuss it by our primary understanding of the theme; renewal of the church's life as a necessary precondition for its numerical growth. What do we mean by this newness of life?

I think we should understand it in the radical eschatological context of the Bible. Newness in the biblical sense is not the gradual development or amendment of an old thing toward a better quality. It must be understood ontologically as the substitution of one kind of life by a completely different one. The Uppsala theme was taken from Revelation 21:5: "Behold, I make all things new." In my understanding, the way in which this verse was made use of in describing the participation of the church in the present socio-political quests to bring about better conditions for the human life was a misinterpretation of the word. For in Revelation 21:5 it clearly means the totally new creation of heaven and earth as a sovereign act of God Himself at the end.

But the introduction of the new eschatological life does not begin only after this present age in which we live has passed away. The decisive message of the New Testament is that in Jesus Christ God has already made a beginning of the new things to come. He is the new man who is the true image of God over against the old man who after the fall of Adam is living a life marked by spiritual and physical corruption, a life unto death. Jesus through His atoning death and His resurrection has also become the beginner of a new mankind. Through vital contact with Him we are to be transformed into His image and to share in His divine life. This new mankind consists by no means of all human beings born after the resurrection of Christ. The new mankind are those who through a dramatic process of faith, repentance and baptism have become born again into His life and who have become mystically linked with Him. It is the church who is the body of Christ, and the new life is manifested both individually in her members and also corporately in their *koinonia*. In the church of Christ men already encounter under the conditions of this world the reality of the new life to come. Besides the convincing power of the proclaimed Gospel it is the fascination of this new life which attracts non-Christians to become converted and which decisively contributes to the growth of the church. The nature of this life is divine, sacrificial love — love of God and love of fellow men.

It is obvious that I have been speaking of the church in the theological sense as the New Testament describes it and not in the sociological sense as we actually find it. One great cause of conflict between present ecumenical missiology and the more conservative understanding of mission is that in the recent ecumenical documents the church is almost exclusively referred to in the sociological sense. Therefore it is usually scolded and undervaluated in its significance. I do, however, also clearly recognize the contrast between the church in the theological and in the empirical sense. I ascribe this contrast to the eschatological tension in this interim period between the Ascension and the return of Christ. Martin Luther described it by the formula *simul justus et peccator*. This means that the church constantly must be admonished to become in her behavior what in Christ she already is. Paul charges the Ephesians "to be renewed in the spirit of your mind and that ye put on the new man which after God is created in righteousness and true holiness" (4:24).

This means any church in order really to be the Church needs a constant revival or transformation. This can be brought about only by a new unification with Jesus Christ through the means of grace and through becoming obedient to her commission to witness and to serve, sometimes also to suffer with Christ. We have seen that a new love for the Bible is often the foundation of a growing church and that a new concern for the troubled life of people is its outward manifestation. The two aspects belong together as breathing in and breathing out.

III

Finally, we have to clarify the relationship between a growing church (growing both in maturity and numbers) and the renewal of society. I do not believe that we can speak of the renewal of society in the same sense as of the renewal of the church, because the society belongs to a passing order of this present world, the church — as the body of Christ — belongs to the eternal order of the world to come.

But on a different level the society can participate or benefit from the renewal of the church and thereby manifest signs of the coming kingdom of God. Here we have clearly to distinguish between a society which is basically composed of Christians and a society where Christians form a minority. I stated that the new life is basically an eschatological concept. Its experience here is mediated through a personal, vital connection with Jesus Christ. Since man is a social or political being as well, his becoming a Christian must necessarily be felt in all his social relations. Therefore a church which can count on most citizens of a society as its practicing and convinced members, should be able to a high degree to transform its society by the commandments of God which are revitalized by Christian love.

If, however, a church remains or again is reduced to a minority group in a pluralistic society, it can still make a contribution toward the moral change or at least the moral preservation of such a society, although not always. Think of the story of Lot in Sodom! But normally the church can put forward by a clear witness ethical ideas which as such appeal to the natural conscience even of non-Christians, and the church or individual Christians can take a lead in putting such ideas into practice through *Koinonia* and *Diakonia*.

But the retaining of ethical standards demands personal spiritual power. Thus it becomes obvious again that the moral change of a society depends on the real Christians who have received and who are demonstrating such spiritual power. From there follows a direct relevance of numerical church growth for the renewal of a society. Such Christian contribution toward social renewal does not of course take place automatically by the mere being there of the church. It rather depends on the degree in which the church becomes the Church and is able to direct and to empower its members toward social involvement.

8.

EXCERPTS FROM THE REPORTS, RECOMMENDATIONS, AND
RESOLUTIONS OF THE GENERAL ASSEMBLY OF THE CWME
FROM 9-12 JANUARY 1973

A. From Committee B, "Evangelization and Relations."

(From *Bangkok Assembly 1973*, pp. 17-21.)

● ● ●

B) Guidelines for the Evangelism Secretary

It was agreed that the following report on guidelines for the Evangelism
Secretary be accepted.

Evangelism within the ecumenical movement has come to be understood
as "a dimension of the total activity of the Church" so that "everything
the Church does is of evangelizing significance" (Evanston). Thus the
thrust of evangelism, within WCC structures, cannot be confined to one
particular desk. Rather the role of the Secretary on Evangelism should be
an enabling and a catalytic one. His special tasks should be:

(1) To study structures and situations, movements and models
— outside churches
— within churches
— within the WCC
— where creative communication of salvation takes place;

(2) to share the results of such studies with different regional and
denominational groups and with other programs within the WCC structures, through all appropriate media (e.g., the Monthly Letter on Evangelism);

(3) in a process of "action-reflection" to relate theologically such developments to the biblical message of the present and coming kingdom of
God, thus helping the churches to overcome the traditional giver-receiver
structures in evangelism, and to recognize their own need of salvation in
Christ;

(4) to give special attention to new ways of communication which
imply a sharing of new life rather than of abstract statements on salvation.

E) Relationships With Conservative Evangelicals

The Assembly recommends that

(1) The CWME continue to press efforts at all levels to understand the
concerns and consider the implications of the performance in mission of
conservative evangelicals both within and without the membership of the
WCC, and to remain in contact with them.

(2) The CWME offer its services and make itself available to the Congress of World Evangelization to be convened in Lausanne, July, 1974.

(3) The CWME share the experience of the Bangkok Conference with conservative evangelicals.

F) Relationships With Pentecostals and Independent Churches

Recognizing the contributions and growth of Pentecostal and independent churches and charismatic movements within certain churches, the Assembly recommends that CWME give special attention to such churches and movements with the aim of learning from their experience and sharing with them the insights and experiences of the ecumenical family.

B. From Committee C, "Partnership."

(From *Bangkok Assembly 1973*, pp. 22-25.)

• • •

II. Education for Mission

After accepting an amendment by Dr. Carl Hallencreutz the report of the Committee with its two recommendations was *adopted*.

Education for mission programs, leading to participation in God's mission, must take place at all levels — congregational, theological training, national and regional. The following points should be included.

(1) It should be international in scope.

(2) A renewed understanding of the Bible from the viewpoint of the community of the oppressed is needed.

(3) It is important to sensitize people to world situations — economic, political, cultural and spiritual.

4) Missionaries need to be trained for mobility, moving on when their particular task in one place is completed.

(5) Missionaries also need to become open and flexible and able to learn through dialogue in different situations.

(6) Education must be by involvement and participation.

(7) Dialogue is an integral part of education.

• • •

III. Ecumenical Sharing of Personnel

B) Call for a Moratorium

One of the proposals to develop new patterns of relationships is that there should be a moratorium on the sending of funds and personnel to particular churches for a period of time. The intention is that churches requesting such a moratorium might have an opportunity to work with their own resources to find their own selfhood and identity. Churches no longer able to send money and personnel will be freed from the traditional, institutionalized missionary enterprise to use these resources for new approaches to education for mission amongst their own people. They will also be freed to give financial support to those struggling for freedom from unjust and dehumanizing systems perpetuated by dominant nations and bodies.

The consequence of a moratorium in a particular situation could be the opening up of new styles of relationship, of mature partnership accomplished through consultation and carried out within a process of continuing reflection together.

Of particular significance is the set of guidelines prepared by Section II on whether a foreign mission agency should withdraw from an unjust situation where the majority is dominated by a powerful minority. The issue is highlighted by the withdrawal of the White Fathers from Mozambique. It is relevant also over a broader field of politically and economically unjust situations.

The moratorium idea must be seriously considered in some situations as possibly offering the breakthrough which we are looking for. At the same time a number of questions inevitably arise in any discussion of this proposal:

(a) Does it mean breaking off relationships and isolating churches from one another? Churches are not related to one another only in the sending and receiving of funds and professional missionaries. Many churches enjoy fraternal relationships without any such exchange taking place. Furthermore, there is a constant exchange of Christian lay people who work or study in countries other than their own. Their presence in the congregation can be a missionary presence and a symbol of the ecumenical fellowship.

(b) Who takes the initiative in calling for the moratorium? If a mission agency does so, is this not a new form of imperialism? It would be preferable for the initiative to be taken by the two churches in consultation with other churches in the area concerned.

(c) How will the sending church express its missionary calling if it is deprived of its traditional avenues of work? One answer is that it may discover neglected missionary opportunities in its own country. As for the financial resources diverted from the former channels, there are many potential uses for these, such as projects and programs of development, education for mission in the new context, including education for development and justice, neglected areas of mission in the nation, etc.

Recommendations

(1) That CWME urge, and where possible assist, missionary agencies to examine critically their involvement as part of patterns of political and economic domination, and to reevaluate the role of personnel and finance at their disposal in the light of that examination.

(2) That CWME urge, and where possible assist, missionary agenices to evaluate critically to what extent and in what ways their patterns of

missionary engagement reflect cultural imperialism or involve indiscriminating cultural imposition on churches with which they are related, and what are the consequences for the selfhood identity and mission of these churches.

(3) That CWME provide study papers for discussion of the moratorium proposal as a possible strategy of mission in certain situations as well as information on case studies.

(4) That CWME request mission agencies through its affiliated Councils and churches to provide funds for the strengthening of Regional Councils. . . .

C. From Committee D, "Studies and Publications."
(From *Bangkok Assembly 1973*, p. 31f.)

•   •   •

V. The World Council of Churches and the Peoples' Republic of China

Committee D had been asked to consider a proposal made in the Conference on a study of China. Dr. Johnson presented a prepared statement. This was fully discussed and a number of amendments were proposed, some of which were accepted on behalf of the Committe by its chairman and secretary. A motion to table the statement, made by Fr. Thomas Stransky, was defeated 35 to 21. It was finally agreed that the following statement on the World Council of Churches and the Peoples' Republic of China be adopted:

At a time when the People's Republic of China, embracing about one quarter of the world's population, has moved into a new participation in world affairs, we are reminded of our need as Christians for awareness and understanding of developments in that country.

There are several areas of specific responsibility for the churches:

(1) the need for increasing relationships between the people of China and the people of other lands;

(2) the need for openness of contact between Christians of China and Christians of other lands, as and when Christians of China may initiate it;

(3) the urgent need for knowledge and understanding of Chinese thought in the context of dialogue with people of living ideologies throughout Asia;

(4) the need for a theological and ethical understanding of the transformation of Chinese society and its implications for other societies.

It is noted that a number of national and confessional bodies have begun programs designed to develop a better understanding of contemporary society in China. It is urged therefore that the WCC Executive Committee consider ways to provide, in consultation with the East Asia Christian Conference, guidance and coordination for these various programs.

9

THE FRANKFURT POSITION PAPER

A Position Paper on the World Mission Conference held from 29 December to 12 January 1973, in Bangkok, from the Theological Convention (Theologischer Konvent) and the Frankfurt Mission Convention (Frankfurter Missions-konvent) of the Conference of Confessing Fellowships in the Protestant Church of Germany. *

The Conference of Confessing Fellowships at the meetings of its steering committee, the Theological Convention, and the Frankfurt Missionary Convention from 28 February to 2 March 1973, has busied itself in studying the course and the results of the World Mission Conference in Bangkok. It is issuing the following declaration regarding this conference.

I. Expectations have not been fulfilled

The theme, "Salvation Today," had given rise to the hope in many Christians throughout the whole world that the Commission for World Mission and Evangelism (CWME) of the World Council of Churches would once again place the deliverance from sin and guilt won by the propitiatory sacrifice of our Savior Jesus Christ at the heart of its missionary message. Since the salvation or lostness of the world is dependent upon this, both now and at His return, the most important thing Bangkok should have done would have been to issue a renewed and powerful call to all churches to declare together the message of the kingdom to all peoples (Matt. 24:14; Mark 13:10). This did not happen.

II. Causes for serious consideration

(1) Instead, at the conference as well as in its official reports an alien understanding of salvation was presented under the influence of contemporary ideas. It has separated itself greatly from biblical foundations. Even the results of the "God-is-dead" theology and the Maoist Cultural Revolution were described as expressions of God's saving activity in world history.

---

* The influence of Bangkok began very soon to be noticeable in all levels of the church through the reports and evaluations that have been systematically distributed. The Conference of Confessing Fellowships considered it therefore of unconditional importance to rapidly take a position on this event and press for a clarification of relevant matters. The bases of the following discussion were the resolutions of the World Conference at Bangkok published in the Ecumenical Press Service of 18 January 1973, the "Letter to the Churches," as well as an eyewitness report by the president of the Theological Convention, Prof. Dr. Peter Beyerhaus (*idea*, No. 11/73 of 12 March 1973, p. 1).

(2) The clarification of the fundamental crisis in missions through a consultation of leading theologians of the various commitments from throughout the world to be called as soon as possible was proposed at the beginning and end of the conference. Yet this effort, concerning an issue which has been particularly distressing since the 1968 Uppsala Conference, was consciously hindered by the conference leadership.

(3) Particularly distressing is the resolution of the General Assembly to recommend to the churches of the West a temporary moratorium in the sending of missionaries and money to the churches of the Third World — that is, to the extent that they request this. Just as alarming is the recommendation to use the money saved by this expedient for new ways of mission education among the Christians in the West as well as for the support of militant liberation movements. We judge this to be a betrayal of the missionary mandate which is valid until the return of Jesus Christ: "Go ye into all the world, and preach the gospel to every creature" (Mark 16:15).

III. Our requests

(1) In light of the fact that a four-member delegation of the German Protestant Missions Council participated with full voting privileges at the General Assembly of the CWME in Bangkok, we ask the Council to tell us unambiguously whether it approves or rejects the recommendation of the CWME for a moratorium.

(2) We request the mission societies and church missionary agencies that are represented in the German Protestant Missions Conference to publicly announce their positions on the questionable assertions of the Bangkok Report, and especially the recommendation for a moratorium. This is of extreme importance for the preservation of trusted relationships between Protesant Christians and the missions agencies as well as for the decisions by individual Christians regarding their further support of missions.

(3) Finally, we ask all Christians to be very critical in evaluating the reports and results from Bangkok, including the "Letter to the Churches," that are being spread with such great diligence and not to let themselves be deceived by the familiar biblical phrases that are used, for the true character of these publications is actually contrary to the Gospel. To aid in this effort the Conference of Confessing Communions will publish in the near future a searching report on the Bangkok Conference with a biblical-theological interpretation of its documents. We ask the congregations and their members not to grow weary in their sacrifices for missions. But we also ask them not to support any mission which does not do its work according to biblical standards and which does not firmly disassociate itself from the false understanding of salvation represented in Bangkok as, for example, the Frankfurt Declaration has already done.

Adopted by the Theological Convention and the Frankfurt Mission Convention of the Conference of Confessing Fellowships in the Protestant Church of Germany.

Frankfurt am Main. 2 March 1973.

APPENDIX

REFERENCES TO FURTHER PUBLICATIONS ON THE EIGHTH WORLD MISSION CONFERENCE IN BANGKOK

I have considered, with a few exceptions, only the German and most important English language publications. They are divided as follows:

I. Books
II. Special journal issues devoted to the conference
III. Individual essays
IV. Individual documents

Within these divisions the following distinction has been made:

A. Preparatory material
B. Reports and commentary on the conference.

Official documents are ranged at the head of each division.

I.A

Thomas Wieser, ed., *Biblical Perspectives on Salvation. A Selection of Biblical Texts, With Comments.* Geneva, 1972 (official)

Salvation Today and Contemporary Experience (an anthology). Geneva: WCC, Unified Program for "Faith and Witness," Commission for World Mission and Evangelism, 1972 (official)

From Mexico City to Bangkok (Report of the Commission on World Mission and Evangelism, 1963-1972); Geneva: WCC, 1972 (official)

Salvation Today. Bangkok, 29 December 1972 to 8 January 1973. (Program schedule for the conference); Geneva: WCC Publication Office, November, 1972 (official)

H. J. Margull and St. J. Samartha, eds., *Dialog mit anderen Religionen. Material aus der ökumenischen Bewegung* [Dialogue With Other Religions. Material From the Eumenical Movement]; Frankfurt: Verlag Lembeck, 1972

Carl F. Hallencreutz, ed., *Verkligen fria — Frihet och Frälsning* [Truly Free — Freedom and Salvation], (Two study books for Bangkok); Falun/Sweden, 1972

I.B.

Bangkok Assembly 1973 (Minutes and Report of the Assembly of the Commission on World Mission and Evangelism of the World Council of Churches, 31 December 1972 and 9-12 January 1973); Geneva: WCC 1973 (official report)

Das Heil der Welt heute, Ende oder Beginn der Weltmission? [Salvation Today: End or Beginning of World Missions?] (Documents of the World Mission Conference, Bangkok, 1973). Edited for the WCC by Philip Potter, the German edition by Thomas Wieser; Stuttgart/Berlin: Kreuz Verlag, 1973 (official report)

K. Viehweger, *Samudhprakarn, Kilometer 31* [*Samut Prakan: Kilometer 31*] (A Report from Asia concerning the World Mission Conference on Salvation Today). Hamburg: Siebernstern Taschenbuch Verlag, 1973

H. J. Margull and J. Freytag, eds., *Keine Einbahnstrassen: Von der Westmission zur Weltmission* [*No One-Way Streets: From the West Mission to World Mission*]. Stuttgart/Korntal: Evangelischer Missionsverlag, 1973

Prof. Dr. J. Verkuyl, *Jezus Christus, de bevrijder* [*Jesus Christ the Liberator*] (A Consideration of the World Conference on Mission and Evangelism in Bangkok.) With the collaboration of A. H. van den Heuvel, M. M. Thomas, J. Th. Witrliet, 1973

Ralph Winter, ed., *The Evangelical Response to Bangkok*. Pasadena: William Carey Library, 1973

II.A

International Review of Mission (WCC Publications Office).
October 1968 — *Salvation Today*;
January 1970 — *Edinburgh 1910 and Now*;
January 1971 — *Humanization and Mission*;
January 1972 — *Salvation Today II*;
July 1972 — *Identity and Community*;
For Section I:
October 1970 — *Faithful Dialogue*. (official documents)

Ecumenical Press Service (Geneva, WCC).
Monthly publication: May 1971, pp. 8-10.
October 1972, pp. 7-9
December 1972, pp. 3-7.

H. H. Ulrich, ed., "Studienmaterial zur Weltmissionskonferenz 1972/73" [Study Material for the World Mission Conference 1972/73], *Studienreihe für Verkündigung und Gemeindeaufbau Heft 2*; Gladbeck: Schriftenmissionsverlag, 1972

II.B

International Review of Mission (official document).
April 1973 — Meeting in Bangkok.

Ecumenical Press Service (Geneva, WCC).
Monthly publication: January 1973, pp. 3-16.
April 1973, pp. 3-7.
Weekly publication: 18 January 1973.

German Protestant Press Service — Documents (Frankfurt/Main: Zentralredaktion) 15 February 1973: A selection of texts in preliminary translation, summarizing the resolutions of the General Assembly.

26 March 1973: *The World Mission Conference in the Mirror of Criticism.* With contributions from: P. Beyerhaus, H. Burkle, P. G. Buttler, E. Castro, H. Class, W. Gengnagel, G. Hoffmann, Ph. Potter, M. M. Thomas, Th. Wieser.

Christianity Today, "Dateline Bangkok," 30 March 1973. (Articles, etc. by Harold Lindsell and Peter Beyerhaus)

John V. Taylor. "Bangkok and after," *CMS News-Letter*, April 1973. (London, Church Missionary Society)

Evangelical Missions Quarterly, vol. 9, no. 3 (Spring 1973). (Special issue on "Salvation Today" with articles by C. Peter Wagner, Jack F. Shepherd, Arthur F. Glasser, and Peter Beyerhaus. Wheaton)

Lebendige Gemeinde, "Mission — bis Jesus kommt" ["Missions — Until Jesus Comes"], no. 15 (May 1973). (Articles, etc. by R. Scheffbuch and F. Grünzweig)

National Christian Council Review, "Salvation Today," March 1973. (National Christian Council of India)

der überblick, "Salvation Today," no. 1 (March 1973). Stuttgart: Dienste in Ubersee, 1973)

III.A

"Salvation Today: Issues for Further Study," *Study Encounter*, no. 4 (1969), pp. 209, 210 (official document)

Heinrich Balz, "Das Heil der Welt — heute. Vorschau auf die ökumenische Weltmissionskonferenz in Bangkok 1972-73" [*Salvation Today. A Preview of the Ecumenical World Mission Conference in Bangkok 1972-73*], *Informationsbrief der Bekenntnisbewegung* "Kein anderes Evangelium," no. 36 (December 1972), pp. 17-31

Peter Beyerhaus, "Die Geister scheiden sich" ["*The Spirits are Dividing*"], *Evangelische Kommentare*, December 1972, pp. 741ff.

——————, "Salvation Today!" *Christianity Today*, no. 27 (October 1972), pp. 49f.

Donald McGavran, "Salvation Today?" *Church Growth Bulletin*, September 1972, pp. 263-266

Walter Hollenweger, "Seven Words on Salvation Today," *Study Encounter*, no. 1 (1970), pp. 16-25

Jacques Rossel, "Gottes Heil in der Liebe" ["*God's Salvation in Love*"], *Evangelische Missionszeitschrift*, February 1973, pp. 13-23

"'Salvation Today' and Yesterday, and Forever," *Christianity Today*, 22 December 1972, pp. 22f.

Stanley J. Samartha, "Die Grenzen geraten in Unruhe. Im Dialog mit den Religionen und Ideologien" ["The Boundaries are Uneasy. In the Dialogue with Religions and Ideologies"], *Evangelische Kommentare*, 1972, pp. 592-595

H. H. Ulrich, "Beständige Fragen nach dem Heil" ["Constant Questions About Salvation"], *Lutherische Monatshefte*, no. 11 (1972), pp. 596-600

Thomas Wieser, "Welches Heil verkündigt die Mission?" ["Which Salvation does Missions Proclaim?"], *Evangelische Kommentare*, December 1972, pp. 735ff.

_____, "Das Heil der Welt heute" [*Salvation Today*], *Das Wort in der Welt*, 1971, pp. 114f.

III.B

U. Betz, "Die Scheidung der Geister beginnt. Nachdenkliches zur Welmissionskonferenz in Bangkok" ["The Division of the Spirits Begins. Things to Think About Concerning the World Mission Conference in Bangkok"], *idea*, no. 11 (12 March 1973), pp. iii-v

P. Beyerhaus, "Eindrücke von der Weltmissionkonferenz in Bangkok" ["Impressions of the World Mission Conference in Bangkok"], *idea*, no. 3 (15 January 1973), p. 1

_____, "Bangkok — Salvation Today?" *EFAC* — Bulletin, no. 10 (March 1973). (London, Evangelical Fellowship in the Anglican Communion)

_____, "Die Weltkonferenz von Bangkok: Persönliche Eindrücke" ["The World Conference of Bangkok: Personal Impressions"], *Theologische Beitrage* (Brockhaus), no. 3 (1973), pp. 120-142

H. Blauert, "Bangkok — Ende einer Missionsera — Anfang der Weltmission" ["Bangkok — End of a Mission Era — Beginning of World Mission"], *Der Ruf, Berliner Missionberichte*, no. 2 (1973), pp. 41-44

P. G. Buttler, "Bangkok — Ein Anfang am Ende der westlichen Missionsepoche" ["Bangkok — A Beginning of the End to the Western Missionary Epoch"], *Okumenische Rudschau* 22, no. 2 (1973), pp. 257-267

Helmut Class, "In Bangkok erlebt und notiert" ["Experiences and Observations in Bangkok"], *Evangelisches Gemeindeblatt für Württemberg*, no. 9-11 (4, 11, and 18 March 1973)

_____, "Hypotheken der Mission ["Mortgaging Missions"], *Evangelische Kommentare*, no. 3 (1973), pp. 150f.

Eberhard le Coutre, "Katalysator für das Heilswerk. Ammerkungen zur ökumenischen Konferenz in Bangkok" ["Catalyst for the Work of Salvation. Observations on the Ecumenical Conference in Bangkok"], *Lutherische Monatshefte*, no. 3 (1973), pp. 114-118

——————, "Moratorium und kein Ende. Zum Striet nach Bangkok" ["Moratorium and not an End. On the Dispute at Bangkok"], *Evangelischer Pressedienst*, no. 12 (21 March 1973), pp. 1-4

W. Gengnagel, "Ende oder Neubeginn?" ["End or New Beginning?"), *EMS Berichte und Nachrichten, Gemeinsame Schritte*, no. 2 (1973), pp. 3, 4

——————, "Heil in einer spannungsvollen Welt — Was hat die Weltmissionskonferenz in Bangkok gebracht?" ["Salvation in a World filled with Tension. What did the World Mission Conference in Bangkok Accomplish?"], *Stuttgarter Evang. Sonntagsblatt*, no. 12 (1973), pp. 10f.

H. W. Gensichen, "Bangkok und die Entwicklungsfrage" ["Bangkok and the Question of Development"], *epd Entwicklungspolitik*, no. 2 (1973), pp. 13-16

Hans-Joachim Girock, "Können diese westlichen Kirchen geheilt werden?" ["Can these Western Churches be Saved?"], *Mitteilungen fur Mitarbeiter der Evangelischen Landeskirche in Baden*, no. 2 (1973), pp. 23-26

Arthur F. Glasser, "Zwiespältige Eindrücke" ["Conflicting Impressions"], *idea*, no. 14 (1973), pp. vii-viii

Donald Hoke, "Salvation Isn't the Same Today," *Christianity Today*, 2 February 1973, pp. 37ff.

W. J. Hollenweger, "Professor Unrat geht nach Bangkok. Die Weltmissionskonferenz oder Variationen zu einem Roman" ["Prof. Unrat goes to Bangkok. The World Mission Conference or Variations on a Novel"], *Evangelische Kommentare*, no. 3 (1973), pp. 146-149

Ch. v. L. Imhoff, "Das neue ökumenische Gesicht; Asien und Afrika prägten die Bangkok-Konferenz" ["The New Ecumenical Look; Asia and Africa Leave Their Mark on the Bangkok Conference"], *Lutherische Monatshefte*, no. 2 (1973), pp. 63-66

——————, "Bangkok. Für ein neues Missionsverständnis" ["Bangkok. For a New Understanding of Mission"], *LWB-Informationen*, no. 4 (1973), pp. 2-7

Harold Lindsell, "Schlussfolgerungen aus Bangkok" ["Conclusions from Bangkok"], *idea*, no. 15 (1973), p. iii

Michael Mildenberger, "HEIL HEUTE" [Salvation Today], *Sonderdruck der Evangelischen Zentralstelle für Weltanschauungsfragen* (Stuttgart), April 1973, pp. 1-9

——————, "Die Anstösse von Bangkok" ["The Initiatives of Bangkok"], *Dt. Pfarrerblatt*, no. 7 (1973), pp. 244-247

J. Moltmann, "Bangkok 1973 — Eine Mission an uns" ["Bangkok 1973 — A Mission to Us"], *Evangelische Theologie*, vol. 33, no. 2 (March/April, 1973)

F. C. Schilling, "Abschied vom weissen Missionar" ["The Disengagement of White Missionaries"], *Deutsche Zeitung/Christ und Welt*, 19 January 1973, p. 8

Ernst Sommer, "Deutscher Streit um Bangkok" ["German Dispute over Bangkok"], *Wort und Weg, Sonntagsblatt der Evang. Methodistischen Kirche*, vol. 6, no. 19 (13 May 1973), p. 298f.

M. M. Thomas, "Teilnehmen an der Befreiung. Ein Inder über das Heil und den Auftrag der Kirche" ["Participation in Liberation. An Indian Speaks on Salvation and the Mission of the Church"], *Lutherische Monatshefte*, no. 2 (1973), pp. 82-85

H. H. Ulrich, "Feier und Verkundigung des Heils. Bilanz der Weltmissionskonferenz" ["Celebration and Proclamation of Salvation. Balance at the World Mission Conference"], *Das Missionarische Wort* (Gladbeck), March/April 1973, supplement 3

_____, "Mission im Lernprozess — zur Diskussion uber Bangkok" ["Mission in the Learning Process — to the Discussion Concerning Bangkok"], *Das Missionarische Wort*, no. 3 (1973), pp. 98-101

Klaus Viehweger, "Was kam dabei heraus?" ["What Were the Results of That?"], *Deutsches Allgemeines Sonntagsblatt*, 21 January 1973

_____, "Mission fängt in der Kirche an" ["Mission begins in the Church"], *Deutsches Allgemeines Sonntagsblatt*, 14 January 1973

C. Peter Wagner, "Horizontale stärker betont als Vertikale" ["The Horizontal Dimension Stressed More Than the Vertical"], *idea*, no. 14 (1973), pp. iv-v

IV.A

Einheit von Zeugnis und Dienst ["Unity of Witness and Service"]. (A Resolution of the Protestant-Mekan-Jesus-Church in Ethiopia.) In *Jahrbuch Evangelische Mission 1973* (Hamburg: Deutsche Evangelische Missionshilfe, 1973), pp. 248-255

Kritik an der westlichen Mission und Weltmissionskonferenz 1972 ["A Critique of Western Missions and the World Mission Conference of 1972"]. In *Das Wort in der Welt*, no. 10 (1972), p. 12

Moratorium für die Aussendung von Missionaren? ["A Moratorium on the Sending of Missionaries?"]. In *Das Wort in der Welt*, no. 5 (October 1972), p. 143

IV.B

Erste Beschlüsse der Kommission für Weltmission und Evangelisation nach Bangkok ["First Resolutions of the Commission for World Mission and Evangelism at Bangkok"]. *Ecumenical Press Service*, 18 January 1973, pp. 4f.

"Weltkongress für Evangelisation wird Gegenstück zu Bangkok" ["The World Congress of Evangelism becomes Antithetical at Bangkok"]. (An interview with Prof. Peter Beyerhaus.) In epd ZA, no. 8 (11 January 1973), pp. 6, 7

"Mission ist der Sache nach keineswegs überholt"] Mission as such Is by No Means Outmoded"]. (An interview with Rev. Ulrich.) In epd ZA, no. 10 (15 January 1973), pp. 6, 7

Im Zeichen von Bangkok ["In the Sign of Bangkok"]. In Informationsblatt der Kirchlichen Sammlung um Bibel und Bekenntnis, vol. 20, no. 3 (March 1973), pp. 44f.

P. Beyerhaus. "Begründung der Frankfurter Stellungnahme vom 2.3.73 zur Bangkok-Konferenz" ["The Motivation for the Frankfurt Position Paper of 2 March 1973, on the Bangkok Conference"]. A mimeographed memorandum in the service of the Conference of Confessing Communions in the Protestant Churches of Germany. Tübingen, April 1973

GLOSSARY OF ABBREVIATIONS, THEOLOGICAL AND FOREIGN PHRASES

absolution — the imparting of forgiveness

animateur — inciter, a specialist in the group dynamics process

cantus firmus ecumenicus — the principal melody in the many-voiced choir of the ecumenical movement

CWME — Commission of World Mission and Evangelism of the World Council of Churches

Dhamma — Buddhist instructions concerning the way of salvation

dialectical — thinking in antitheses

eo ipso — from itself, self-evidently

evangelical — Anglo-saxon designation for orthodox pietists

ex cathedra — with a plentitude of power, infallible

exegetical — the scientific interpretation of the Bible

Happy Hall — a building in the conference center at Bangkok

horizontalist — someone to whom relations among men are most important (opposite: verticalist)

idea — Information Service of the Protestant Alliance

IRM — International Review of Mission

kerygmatic — concerning the proclamation of the Gospel

koinonia — (church) fellowship

Kyrie eleison — Prayer in the worship service, "Lord, have mercy!"

Luthuli Foundation — named after Albert John Luthuli, winner of the Nobel Peace Prize of 1961

Messianism — spiritual movement which awaits salvation from a messiah

Mexico City, 1963 — the site of the Seventh World Mission Conference

Nirvana — salvation through "extinction," the highest holiness

Orthodox — (a) correct in belief, (b) the Eastern churches that have been separated from Rome since 1054.

pan-religious — interpreting all things as religious, thoroughly penetrated by religion

Program Unit — one of the three main departments of the World Council of Churches

reflector — a specialist in the group dynamics process

soteriological — having to do with salvation

status quo — conditions as they now are

syncretism — the mixing of different religions

Tripitaka — (Indian) "the three baskets," the principal source of the Buddhist religion

Upanishads — the holy scriptures of Hinduism

Uppsala 1968 — the Fourth General Assembly of the World Council of Churches

verticalist — someone who lays emphasis on the relationship between God and man (opposite: horizontalist)

WCC — The World Council of Churches

Wheaton Congress 1966 — an important gathering of evangelical missionaries in Wheaton, Illinois

Whitby 1947 — the Fourth World Mission Conference

Willingen 1952 — the Fifth World Mission Conference

Xhosa — a South African Negro language

FURTHER BOOKS AND WRITINGS BY PROF. DR. PETER BEYERHAUS

Allen Völkern zum Zeugnis: Biblisch-theologische Besinnung zum Wesen der Mission ["As a Testimony to All Peoples: A Biblical and Theological Consideration on the Essence of Missions"]. R. Brockhaus Verlag, 1972, 144 pp.

Die Grundlagenkrise der Mission ["The Fundamental Crisis in Missions"]. R. Brockhaus Verlag, 1970, 40 pp.

Humansierung — einzige Hoffnung der Welt? ["Humanization — the Only Hope of the World?"] 3rd ed., MKB-Verlag, 1971, 80 pp.

In Ostasien erlebt ["Experiences in East Asia"] Evang. Missionsverlag, 1972, 128 pp.

In der Inselwelt Südostasiens erlebt ["Experiences in the Island World of South East Asia"]. (Continuation of the preceding book.) Evang. Missionsverlag, 1973, 160 pp.

Die Selbständigkeit der jungen Kirchen als missionarisches Problem ["The Independence of Young Churches As a Problem in Missions"]. 3rd ed. Verlag Rhein. Mission, 1967, 393 pp.

The following works have appeared in the series CHRISTUSBEKENNTNIS HEUTE [Confessing Christ Today] of the Verlag der Liebenzeller Mission:

Bibel ohne Heiligen Geist? ["Bible Without the Holy Spirit?"] (No. 5.) 3rd ed., 1970, 24 pp.

Die Versuchungsstunde des Okumenischen Rates: Uppsala 1968 im Spiegel seines biblischen Leitwortes ["The Hour of Temptation for the World Council of Churches: Uppsala 1968 in the Mirror of Its Biblical Theme"]. (Nos. 6/7.) 2nd ed., 1970, 40 pp.

Gemeinschaft in der Kirche — heute? ["Fellowship in the Church — Today?"] (Nos. 8/9.), 1970, 36 pp.

Die Grundlagenkrise der Mission ["The Fundamental Crisis in Missions"]. (Nos. 11/12.) 1970, 40 pp.

Die Wheaton — Erklärung ["The Wheaton Declaration"]. (Basic questions concerning Missions, ed. by Peter Beyerhaus.) (No. 13), 1970, 25 pp.

Rassismus — seine evangeliumsgemässe Uberwindung ["Racism — Overcoming It in Accordance With the Gospel"]. 2nd ed., 1972, 25 pp.

Jesus Christus und die Weltreligionen ["Jesus Christ and the World Religions"]. (No. 15.), 1973, 25 pp.

The following are books by Prof. Beyerhaus which have appeared in English [the first two are not matched with their German originals as their titles are not word-for-word translations of original German titles — trans.]:

Missions — Which Way? Grand Rapids: Zondervan, 1971. (Contemporary Evangelical Perspectives Series.)

Shaken Foundations: Building Mission Theology. Grand Rapids: Zondervan, 1972.

(With Henry C. Lefever). *The Responsible Church and the Foreign Mission.* Grand Rapids: Eerdmans, 1964. (Based on *Die Selbständigkeit der jungen Kirchen als missionarisches Problem.*)